TAJIKISTAN NATIONAL URBAN ASSESSMENT
MAKING THE CASE FOR ACCELERATED URBANIZATION

APRIL 2024

ASIAN DEVELOPMENT BANK

 Creative Commons Attribution 3.0 IGO license (CC BY 3.0 IGO)

© 2024 Asian Development Bank
6 ADB Avenue, Mandaluyong City, 1550 Metro Manila, Philippines
Tel +63 2 8632 4444; Fax +63 2 8636 2444
www.adb.org

Some rights reserved. Published in 2024.

ISBN 978-92-9270-665-4 (print); 978-92-9270-666-1 (PDF); 978-92-9270-667-8 (e-book)
Publication Stock No. TCS240229-2
DOI: http://dx.doi.org/10.22617/TCS240229-2

The views expressed in this publication are those of the authors and do not necessarily reflect the views and policies of the Asian Development Bank (ADB) or its Board of Governors or the governments they represent.

ADB does not guarantee the accuracy of the data included in this publication and accepts no responsibility for any consequence of their use. The mention of specific companies or products of manufacturers does not imply that they are endorsed or recommended by ADB in preference to others of a similar nature that are not mentioned.

By making any designation of or reference to a particular territory or geographic area in this document, ADB does not intend to make any judgments as to the legal or other status of any territory or area.

This publication is available under the Creative Commons Attribution 3.0 IGO license (CC BY 3.0 IGO) https://creativecommons.org/licenses/by/3.0/igo/. By using the content of this publication, you agree to be bound by the terms of this license. For attribution, translations, adaptations, and permissions, please read the provisions and terms of use at https://www.adb.org/terms-use#openaccess.

This CC license does not apply to non-ADB copyright materials in this publication. If the material is attributed to another source, please contact the copyright owner or publisher of that source for permission to reproduce it. ADB cannot be held liable for any claims that arise as a result of your use of the material.

Please contact pubsmarketing@adb.org if you have questions or comments with respect to content, or if you wish to obtain copyright permission for your intended use that does not fall within these terms, or for permission to use the ADB logo.

Corrigenda to ADB publications may be found at http://www.adb.org/publications/corrigenda.

Notes:
In this publication, "$" refers to United States dollars.
ADB recognizes "China" as the People's Republic of China and "Russia" as the Russian Federation.

On the cover: Without a strategy that links economic development to urbanization, Tajikistan will not be able to harness the full potential of its human capital and allow its cities to fulfill their role as engines of growth. The two leftmost photos are by Firuz Safarov, ADB. The five others are by Nozim Kalandarov, ADB.

Cover design by Edith Creus.

Contents

Tables and Figures	v
Acknowledgments	vii
Abbreviations	viii
Measures and Weights	ix
Executive Summary	x
Overall Country Profile	**1**
1.1 Geography, Land Types, and Settlement Patterns	2
1.2 Disasters and Climate Change	3
1.3 Economy	9
1.4 Political History and System of Governance	12
Urban Profile	**14**
2.1 Urbanization Trends	14
2.2 Urban Hierarchy and Settlement Types	15
2.3 Contribution of Cities to the National Economy	19
2.4 Spatial Analysis at the Urban Level	23
2.5 Subsector Assessment	28
2.6 Urban Environment	39
2.7 Urban Governance and Management Profile	40
2.8 Urban Finance Profile	43
Government Policies and External Assistance	**53**
3.1 Government Policies	53
3.2 External Assistance	58
Development Challenges and Priorities	**60**
4.1 Urban Sector Problems	60
4.2 Causes	61
4.3 Priority Issues	63
4.4 Core Problem	67

Making Cities in Tajikistan More Livable — **69**
    5.1 Short Term — 69
    5.2 Medium Term — 78
    5.3 Long Term — 83
    5.4 Applicability and Relevance of Innovative Solutions — 85

Appendixes — **87**
    1 Main Legal Documents on Public Finance Management — 87
    2 Select Urban Projects and Urban-Related Activities of International Financial Institutions — 89

Tables and Figures

Tables

1	Administrative Subdivisions (as of 1 January 2021)	2
2	Urban Population Proportion of Central Asian Countries, 2000, 2007, and 2020 (% of total)	7
3	Administrative and Territorial Divisions	12
4	Urban Population (as of 1 January 2021)	15
5	Classification and Population of Urban Settlements (as of 1 January 2021)	16
6	Urban Population Growth, 2000–2021	17
7	Desk Estimation of the Population in Khujand Agglomeration	18
8	Population Growth Rate in Settlements Around Khujand, 2000–2021	26
9	Registered Vehicles Per 1,000 People, 2000–2018	29
10	Financing Sources of Commissioned Housing and Residential Buildings, 2020	34
11	Ownership of Commissioned Residential Buildings	34
12	Number of Construction Enterprises	35
13	Mortgage Terms in Select Banks in Tajikistan (as of mid-2022)	36
14	Waste Disposal Tariffs in Dushanbe Districts	37
15	Land Use in Dushanbe	40
16	Responsibilities in Public Finance Management (Other Agencies)	44
17	Tax Rates by Type, Size, and Location of Real Estate	46
18	Regional Coefficients Regulating Real Estate Tax Amounts	47
19	Land Tax Rates	48
20	Local Revenues, Quarter 1, 2022 (TJS million)	49
21	Local Activities and Financing Sources	51
22	National Development Strategy Benchmarks	55
23	ADB Cumulative Commitments (as of April 2023)	59
24	Summary of Priority Issues	67
25	State Agencies Responsible for Urban Development	68
26	Proposed Policy Measures and Indicative Investments, Short-Term Scenario (1–5 Years)	76
27	Proposed Policy Measures and Indicative Investments, Medium-Term Scenario (5–10 Years)	81
28	Proposed Policy Measures and Indicative Investments, Long-Term Scenario (10–20 Years)	85

Figures

1	Map of Tajikistan	1
2	Urban Population Centers, 2021	4
3	Population Pyramid, 2021	7
4	Subnational Government Hierarchy	13
5	Map of Khujand Agglomeratio	19
6	Central Asia Regional Economic Cooperation Corridors	22
7	Dushanbe Functional Urban Area	24
8	Khujand and Surrounding Settlements	26
9	Highway and Railway Network and Border Crossings	27
10	Steps in the Urban Planning Process	43
11	Urban Sector Problem Tree	60

Acknowledgments

The National Urban Assessment (NUA) of Tajikistan is part of the regional technical assistance project, Strengthening Urban Investment Planning and Capacity for Project Preparation and Implementation in Central and West Asia, of the Asian Development Bank (ADB).

Designed to provide an overarching analytical framework and strategic context for integrated urban development, the NUA analyzes the urbanization process. It identifies the leading environmental, social, and economic development issues relating to the urban sector and ADB's value addition and new areas of support to make cities more livable, green, competitive, resilient, and inclusive, consistent with ADB's Strategy 2030.

Specifically, the Tajikistan NUA aims to (i) provide a baseline picture of the state of Tajikistan's urban sector and its multiple factors and (ii) define possible urban futures to facilitate ADB's dialogue with the government and future technical and financial support to the sector.

The NUA was prepared by Pablo Vaggione (main author, ADB consultant) and Firuz Kataev (national coordinator, ADB consultant) under the guidance of Shanny Campbell, country director, Tajikistan Resident Mission, ADB; Jingmin Huang, director, Water and Urban Development Sector Office (SG-WUD), Sectors Group, ADB; Heeyoung Hong, principal urban development specialist, SG-WUD, Sectors Group, ADB; and Xijie Lu, urban development specialist, SG-WUD, Sectors Group, ADB.

Muhammadi Boboev and Firuza R. Dodomirzoeva of the Tajikistan Resident Mission contributed to the development and management of the project. Jean Laguerder (ADB consultant) provided editorial support and coordinated the publication process. Marie Charmaine Alcantara and Marcelle Anne Luna Santos of the SG-WUD provided overall administrative support. Rodel Bautista of the Department of Communications and Knowledge Management (DOCK) coordinated DOCK support and DOCK-accredited artists and service providers helped with the various aspects of production.

The report team would like to express its sincere appreciation for the valuable time and inputs given by agencies of the Government of Tajikistan to the preparation of this report.

Abbreviations

ADB	Asian Development Bank
CAC	Committee on Architecture and Construction
CAREC	Central Asia Regional Economic Cooperation
COVID-19	coronavirus disease
DRS	Districts of Republican Subordination
EBRD	European Bank for Reconstruction and Development
FUA	functional urban area
GBAO	Gorno-Badakhshan Autonomous *Oblast* (Mountainous Badakhshan Autonomous Region)
GDP	gross domestic product
GHG	greenhouse gas emissions
IFI	international financial institution
JICA	Japan International Cooperation Agency
MOF	Ministry of Finance
NDS	National Development Strategy
NUA	national urban assessment
PPP	public–private partnership
PRC	People's Republic of China
SNG	subnational government
STKEC	Shymkent–Tashkent–Khujand Economic Corridor
SUE	state unitary enterprise
TAJSTAT	Agency on Statistics under the President of the Republic of Tajikistan
UN	United Nations
UNECE	United Nations Economic Commission for Europe

Measures and Weights

km	kilometer
km²	square kilometer
m	meter
m²	square meter
m³	cubic meter
masl	meters above sea level

Executive Summary

Country Overview

Tajikistan has made significant progress in growing its economy and reducing poverty. The economy grew at an average of 7.0% per year over the last two decades, and the poverty rate fell from 32.0% in 2009 to 13.4% in 2022 (at the international poverty line of $3.65 a day, 2017 purchasing power parity). International migration has been a major driver of this economic advancement. Remittances contributed one-third of the national gross domestic product (GDP) in 2019. Tajikistan has a small economy, with $10.49 billion GDP and $1,054.20 per capita GDP in 2022, the lowest in the Central Asia region. Agriculture generates 24.8% of the GDP, while industry (aluminum, hydropower, food processing, and textiles) contributes 17.0% and services comprise 17.9%.

The National Development Strategy identifies the demographic dividend as an opportunity to increase urbanization. The 2021 census placed Tajikistan's population at 9.51 million. The Agency on Statistics has projected it will reach 16.2 million by 2050. In the next 15 years, the population between the ages of 15 and 64 will comprise 60% of the total. This population age structure presents an opportunity for Tajikistan to benefit from a demographic dividend that it can best harness through urbanization. Several examples worldwide show a positive correlation between a higher degree of urbanization and improved social and economic conditions. A World Bank study that reveals Tajikistan's urban sectors to be almost three times more productive than its rural sectors strengthens the case for greater and accelerated urbanization.

Elevating the quality of growth through urbanization will require a clear pathway. Urban development can be leveraged to alleviate challenges at the national level. But without a strategy that links economic development to urbanization, cities will be constrained from fulfilling their role as engines of growth and main generators of employment. The private sector has been central in creating employment opportunities in urbanizing countries, but its current role in key land-linked sectors of Tajikistan's economy, such as real estate development, construction, and tourism, remains limited. Economic diversification, job opportunities, and the skills and training necessary to develop these sectors will benefit from a national urban strategy and local action plans that make cities more competitive in a land-linked economy. Urban planning and land management systems need to be adjusted to sustain the shift to more competitive urban economies.

The urban population may double by 2050. In 2020, Tajikistan's urban population was 26.2% of the total, making it the least urbanized country in Central Asia. The urbanization rate has hovered at the same level for the past two decades. Emigration, the economic predominance of agriculture, insufficient industrial and services sector jobs, and a lack of affordable urban housing units account for this situation, in addition to the impact that *propiska*, the registration of residence, may have on the local population dynamics. Such impact is yet to be fully analyzed; nevertheless, changes in the existing policy do not seem imminent. To an extent propelled by demographics, the country is forecast to undergo a period of rapid urbanization, with urban dwellers increasing to 43% of the total population by 2050. Considering the Agency on Statistics' forecast of 16.2 million total population, this would imply some 6.8 million people living in cities by 2050, or more than double the absolute number of Tajikistan's urban residents in 2020.

Over half of Tajikistan's urban population lives in the cities of Dushanbe, Khujand, Bokhtar, and Kulob, but their contribution to the national GDP is just 24%. With 916,000 inhabitants in 2022, Dushanbe contributed about 13% of the national GDP. This appears low against comparators such as Yerevan which contributed around 57% to the national GDP, or over four times more. The next three largest cities also contributed relatively low amounts: Khujand comprised 5%, Bokhtar 4%, and Kulob just 2%. A host of factors, including the lack of a clear growth agenda linked to urbanization, insufficient urban jobs, and limited private sector development, have constrained the cities' contribution to economic growth.

Although growth occurs mainly in the fringes of large cities, no agglomeration approach to urbanization is yet to be applied. The fastest population growth seems to occur in intermediate cities with inhabitants numbering between 50,000 and 100,000 that share the labor market of an adjacent larger city, such as Buston, Gafurov, and Guliston (contiguous to Khujand). An agglomeration approach factors in the actual population within a contiguous territory inhabited at urban density levels, regardless of administrative boundaries, in the provision of urban infrastructure and services. However, as Khujand and the adjacent three municipalities previously mentioned are not considered a statistical unit, an agglomeration approach to their development has not been taken by the authorities. A confusing picture of urbanization, which stems from statistical incoherence with the classification of cities set in place by the Urban Planning Code, has also prevented policymakers from fully appreciating the need to apply an agglomeration approach to urban planning and development.

Urban Sector and Institutional Context

The recent national development policy is favorable for urbanization, but further reforms are essential. The National Development Strategy considers factors that link economic development to urbanization and advocates the institutionalization and mainstreaming of an integrated approach to land use policy, urban planning, and property registration in development planning and programming. Nationally, it emphasizes the creation of economic corridors and their integration into regional value chains. Nationwide but with an urban focus, it acknowledges the need to develop the housing market and the real estate sector. The Strategy for the Development of the Construction Industry recognizes the lack of a systematic approach as the most critical issue in urban planning and argues for an update of the Urban Planning Code and the introduction of mechanisms for compliance.

Urban planning and management are constrained by an outdated process. A legacy of the Soviet era, the current urban planning process is highly centralized. The Committee on Architecture and Construction (CAC) is the state agency in charge of planning cities, towns, and other settlements. The Dushanbe-based state unitary enterprise Shahrofar, a design institute under the CAC, is the only entity authorized to prepare urban general plans or master plans, detailed plans, and district plans. Construction permits are issued largely on a case-by-case basis. Digitalization is almost nonexistent, data is scarce and available only at a macro level, and access to information is difficult. There is no structure for stakeholder engagement in the preparation of urban planning documents.

There is no specific budget for urbanization and the financial capacity of subnational governments is inadequate. The Ministry of Finance has no specific budget to support urbanization, which is expected to be covered by sector budgets. However, sectors are unfamiliar with what an integrated approach to urban development requires. Subnational finances are weak and own-source revenues are limited. Property tax, amounting to less than 10% of the total revenues, is the only source assigned to local governments. Foundations for land-based financing do not exist. Municipalities face high operational costs from years of suboptimal asset maintenance. Often, capital expenditures are budgeted without proper regard for recurring expenditures. There are 58 budget organizations including ministries, state committees, and agencies directly reporting to the Ministry of Finance, which fragments the allocation and management of expenditures. While a law on public-private partnership was adopted in 2012, there is no creditworthiness assessment or mechanism to qualify or enable municipalities to borrow.

The housing sector faces key constraints, such as limited stock, lack of affordability, poor maintenance, and weak institutions. In 2011, the housing stock comprised 1.23 million units, equivalent to 163 dwellings per 1,000 inhabitants, the lowest in Central Asia. The CAC does not have official statistics on demand, which impedes getting an accurate picture. The average salary is about $120–$150 per month, while the average cost per square meter of a new building in Dushanbe varies from $500 to $1,000. The 22% interest rate and short tenor of housing mortgages make them inaccessible for most citizens. The stock has been poorly maintained and around 51% of multistory houses and 22% of single-story houses are over 50 years old. Sitting tenants continue to overlook the importance of assuming accountability for housing management. The newly enacted Housing Code aims to address this issue with the creation of tenant associations. A study released by the United Nations Economic Commission for Europe a decade ago identified housing as a largely unfunded mandate. Social affordable housing programs have had negligible impact in the last decade.

The transport sector is a key driver for development but requires a profound transformation to fulfill the role. One of the objectives of the National Development Strategy is to transform Tajikistan into a transport hub, which entails enhancing connectivity through infrastructure, logistics centers, and border terminals. However, the undermaintained transport infrastructure and complex topography lead to high transport costs and limited access to markets and services. The lack of a national long-term spatial development program indicating the location of economic centers impedes a strategic and comprehensive approach to transport sector planning. At an urban scale, an integrated approach to mobility must still be developed, and urban land use and transport planning are disconnected. Meanwhile, the motorization rate more than doubled between 2000 and 2018. Traffic congestion is usually addressed from an automobile perspective. There are no incentives to improve non-motorized mobility, and first and last-mile approaches are not considered. These factors contribute to increasing congestion and are putting cities on a deteriorating air quality pathway. Emissions from vehicles, which doubled in the past decade, are the number one cause of air pollution in Dushanbe and other cities. The increasing rate of motorization is likely to exacerbate these externalities.

Urban public transport is inadequate. Privately run minivans, known as *marshrutkas*, dominate public transport in large cities over buses and trolleys operated by state-owned enterprises. Dushanbe has about 1,550 informally operated *marshrutkas*, and in Khujand, they comprise 80% of the 200,000 daily trips from the urban fringes to the city center. Public transport is characterized by poor service and lack of safety, an old fleet consisting of secondhand imported vehicles, deficient infrastructure with lack of dedicated lanes for public transport, inefficient traffic management and no parking management strategy, lack of transport data, and suboptimal network planning.

Drinking water quality has long been a problem in Tajikistan. The country has abundant water resources, but lacks the facilities to make water potable. Public access to centralized water supply systems is 57% nationally and 91% in urban areas. The aging water supply infrastructure contributes to physical water losses, estimated at 60% in urban areas in 2015. Countrywide, the central water supply service is irregular with several areas having an intermittent supply of 6–8 hours per day. Wastewater and stormwater are not recycled. Tariff collection is limited, and in 2016, only 58% of Tajik households reported paying for drinking water, of which 88% were urbanites. Tajikistan uses 2.61 cubic meters (m^3) of water to realize 1 unit of economic output, or over 20 times the 0.11 m^3 average in North and Central Asia and 0.12 m^3 average in the Asia and Pacific region.

The centralized sewerage system is not accessible to most people and network deficiencies contribute to environmental degradation. The country's sewerage system covers 15% of the population with 53.7% in the cities. In Dushanbe, sewerage services are provided to about 70% of the residents, while the remainder, particularly in newly developed areas, use septic tanks. The sewerage system, built during the Soviet era is in poor condition, about 50% of which in the urban areas is not regularly functioning. The wastewater treatment plant functions poorly and only marginal treatment is achieved, which leads to water contamination. Effluents are discharged to river bodies without proper treatment.

Solid waste management in Tajikistan is deficient and waste generation is expected to triple by 2050. More than 5,500 tons of solid waste per day are generated in Tajikistan's cities. This amount is expected to triple by 2050. Solid waste collection services reach 80% of the urban population on average. In Dushanbe, the waste collection rate is 95% but in Khujand it drops to 32%. Collection points are insufficient and in larger cities, it is not uncommon to find solid waste lying in the open for days. Solid waste is dumped in 72 disposal sites throughout the country. According to the Committee on Environment Protection, one solid waste treatment plant is needed in every region. Besides a general law on waste collection procedures, there is no unified and coherent solid waste management strategy. Policies for the reduction of consumption are at inception stages. Recycling is largely underdeveloped, and public awareness is limited. The municipality-owned waste collection companies operating in Dushanbe and Khujand lack financial resources, capacity, and modern equipment. Tariffs are very low and do not meet operational costs.

Disaster risk reduction is insufficiently mainstreamed into development planning. Tajikistan is highly exposed to several natural hazards such as earthquakes, floods, droughts, avalanches, landslides, and mudslides. Disasters caused by these hazards led to 1,041 casualties and about TJS2 billion in damages in 1997–2013. In 2021, the country ranked 140th out of 182 countries in the climate change preparedness index published by the Notre Dame Global Adaptation Initiative. No government agency is currently directly responsible for disaster preparedness and mitigation. Disaster risk reduction and climate change adaptation are still not mainstreamed into development planning, and disaster risk mapping is only to some extent incorporated as part of land use planning.

Looking Forward

Short term. There is an interest from the Government of Tajikistan to incorporate in the growth agenda a pathway for urban development to capture the demographic dividend. This requires crafting a strategy for urbanization to drive economic development and welfare in Tajikistan. It would entail, at the national level, connecting lagging regions to cities and markets, where services and opportunities are more abundant. At the urban level, applying the functional urban area approach, the direction is to create the conditions for the development of a livable, compact urban model that facilitates the economic efficiency of cities and the provision of infrastructure and public services. Policies and investments will jump-start the trajectory in the context of a transition to market-oriented urban development. Livability-enhancing investments in urban mobility, pilot area-based urban regeneration, public green space, streetscape attractiveness, nature-based solutions, air quality, and smart city applications will spearhead the realization of the vision.

Medium term. The recommendation is to roll out the livable urban development model to a system of cities. This builds upon the policy foundation and the demonstration projects that were the focus of short-term actions and are expected to have created a consensus on and momentum toward urbanization, contributing to the national growth agenda. It requires the development of regional planning and the application of the functional urban area approach in Dushanbe, Khujand, Bokhtar, and Kulob to form clusters of cities. Improvement of connectivity will enable the rural population and those living in smaller cities to access welfare services and employment opportunities. Investments will target transport at cluster scale, logistics facilities, area-based urban regeneration with livable eco-districts, the rollout of smart city applications, as well as measures to strengthen resilience and the introduction of circular economy approaches.

Long term. Tajikistan will have the means to consistently apply its urban model based on livability. Improved national and regional connectivity will enable a functional system of cities and contribute to addressing regional constraints. Human development and equality indicators will improve on the back of a diversified and connected economy, in which activities such as tourism, real estate, and logistics will be on a path to maturity, thus making migration a less attractive alternative. Dushanbe will become a node of regional stature known for its livable, green, and resilient characteristics, its effective planning and governance framework, and the efficiency of its basic municipal services. Successful pilot applications in compact urban development, urban mobility, and smart city solutions, among others, will be scaled up and streamlined into policy, public investment, and business practices. Housing options will be accessible for all income levels in the urban centers of Tajikistan, which can attract a wide variety of economic, social, and cultural activities.

Overall Country Profile

Tajikistan is a landlocked country in the heart of Central Asia. It is the smallest country in Central Asia, with a total area of 143,100 square kilometers (km²) and a total population of 9.51 million (2021 census), of which only 28% lived in urban areas in 2022.[1] Once a part of the Soviet Union, Tajikistan (Figure 1) became independent in 1991.

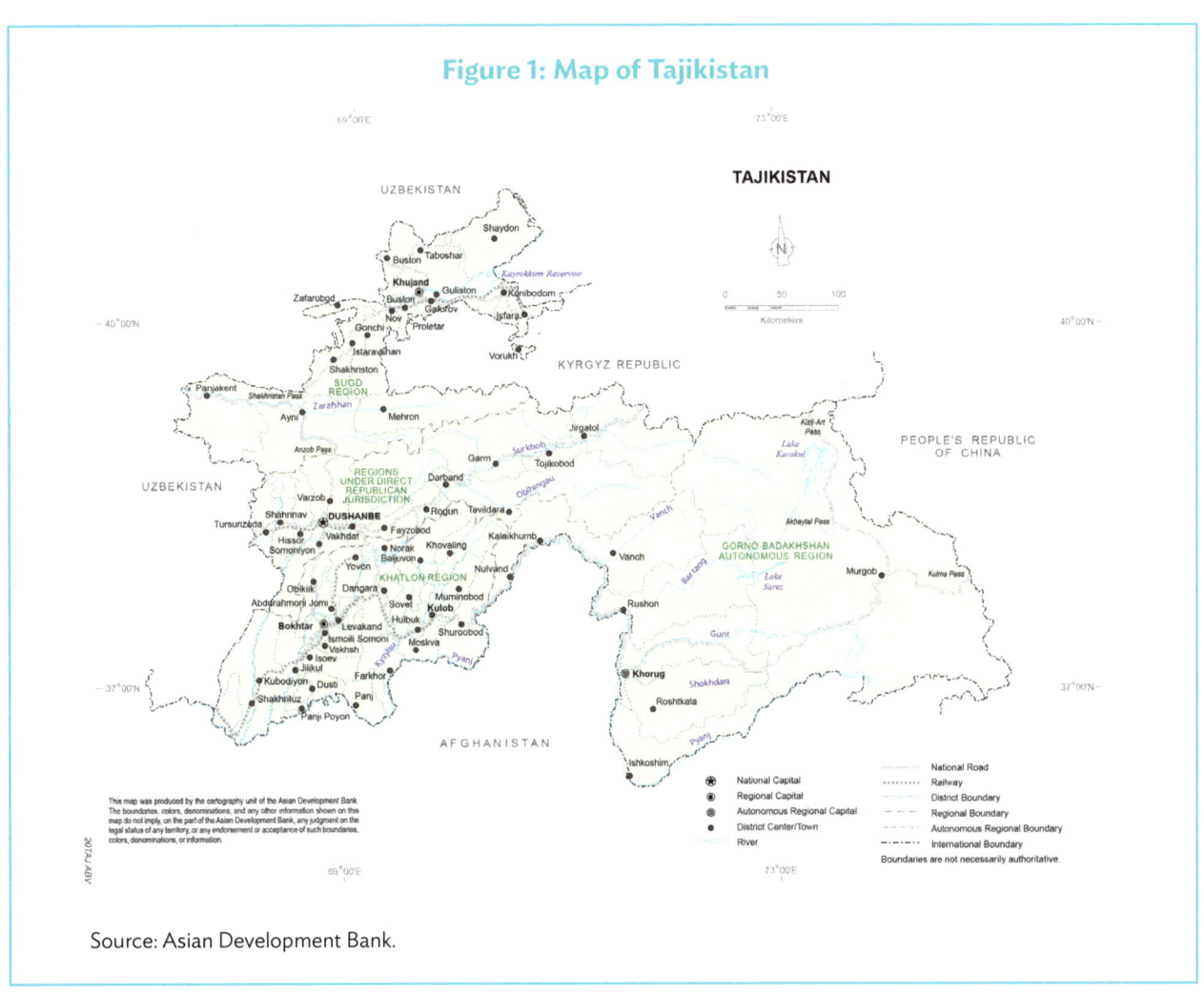

Source: Asian Development Bank.

---

[1] World Bank. Data. Urban Population (% of Total Population) – Tajikistan (accessed 23 August 2023).

Tajikistan is divided into five administrative territories. These territories are the Mountainous Badakhshan Autonomous Region (GBAO); Sugd; Khatlon; the Districts of Republican Subordination (DRS); and the capital, Dushanbe (Table 1). GBAO is the largest subdivision, while the regions of Sugd, Khatlon, and the DRS have slightly varying sizes. Khatlon is the most populated subdivision while GBAO is at the opposite end. The regional administrative centers are Bokhtar for Khatlon, Khujand for Sugd, and Dushanbe for the DRS.

Table 1: Administrative Subdivisions
(as of 1 January 2021)

Territory	Area (1,000 km²)	Share in Total Area (%)	Population (1,000)	Share in Population (%)	Density (persons per km²)
Tajikistan	141.4	100.0	9,506.3	100.0	67.2
Dushanbe	0.1	0.1	880.8	9.3	8,808.0
GBAO	62.9	44.5	231.4	2.4	3.7
Sugd	25.2	17.8	2,753.1	29.0	109.3
Khatlon	24.7	17.5	3,425.5	36.0	138.7
DRS	28.5	20.1	2,215.5	23.3	77.7

DRS = Districts of Republican Subordination, GBAO = Gorno–Badakhshan Autonomous *Oblast* (Mountainous Badakhshan Autonomous Region), km² = square kilometer.

Source: Agency on Statistics under the President of the Republic of Tajikistan. 2021. *Demographic Yearbook of the Republic of Tajikistan, 30th Anniversary of State Independence, 2021* (available in hard copy only).

1.1 Geography, Land Types, and Settlement Patterns

Tajikistan is almost entirely mountainous. With a territory shaped by the massive mountain ranges of Tien Shan, Alai, and Pamir-Darvoz, about 93% of Tajikistan is mountainous.[2] The ranges have elevations reaching 7,495 meters above sea level (masl), the highest in Central Asia. The country has five natural zones, with climates ranging from dry subtropics in the lowlands and plains (400–500 masl) to areas of perpetual snow (5,500–7,400 masl).[3] The mountain ranges are the source of numerous tributaries that flow into Syr Darya, Panj, and Vakhsh, Tajikistan's main rivers.

Less than 7% of Tajikistan's territory consists of relatively flat terrain. Roughly 34% (4.7 million hectares [ha]) of the country's land is agricultural, 77% (2.8 million ha) of which is pastureland. Total arable land fluctuates (856,000 ha in 2016; 837,900 in

---

[2] G.E. Curtis, ed. 1996. *Tajikistan: A Country Study*. Washington: GPO for the Library of Congress; and Asian Development Bank (ADB). 2016. *Country Partnership Strategy: Tajikistan (2016–2020)*. Manila.

[3] The highest mountain peaks are Ismoili Somoni Peak (formerly Communism Peak, renamed in 2000) with an elevation of 7,495 m; Lenin Peak, with 7,134 m; and Eugeniya Korzhenevskaya Peak, with 7,105 m.

2017; 839,400 in 2018; 844,200 in 2019; and 839,400 in 2020) but averages out to an arable land availability of about 0.09 ha per capita, the lowest in Central Asia[4]—Kazakhstan has 1.58 ha per capita; Turkmenistan has 0.32 ha; the Kyrgyz Republic, 0.2 ha; and Uzbekistan, 0.12 ha.[5] Tajikistan also has the lowest ratio of irrigated land to population in Central Asia; in 2019 it was assessed as food insecure by several United Nations (UN) agencies.[6]

The population distribution is uneven, with over three out of four persons residing on the limited flat land. About 85% of the population resides in valleys, foothills, and low-mountain plains and shares these flatlands with agricultural and industrial activities. The remaining 15% lives in mountainous areas. Historically, the population has concentrated in the valley areas of Hissor in the southwest, where Dushanbe, Bokhtar, and Kulob are; and Fergana in the north, where Khujand is (Figure 2).[7] Khatlon, with 36% of the total population in 2021, is predominantly a lowland area, with cities and rural settlements relatively evenly distributed over valleys. The populations of the DRS (23% of the total), Sugd (29.2%), and Dushanbe (9.2%) are concentrated in non-mountainous areas. The largely mountainous GBAO, with a 2.5% share of the national population, has dispersed rural settlements.

1.2 Disasters and Climate Change

Disaster risk reduction is insufficiently mainstreamed into spatial and overall development planning. Tajikistan is prone to disasters. According to the National Development Strategy (NDS), disasters due to earthquakes and climate-related hazards such as floods, droughts, avalanches, landslides, and mudslides resulted in 1,041 casualties and losses of about TJS2 billion across 1997–2013.[8] Using a composite index to assess climate change vulnerability and readiness, the Notre Dame Global Adaptation Initiative ranked Tajikistan 98th out of 182 countries (130th most vulnerable and 140th most ready) in 2021.[9] No government agency is currently directly responsible for disaster preparedness and risk mitigation. Disaster risk reduction and climate change adaptation are also still not mainstreamed in planning processes, and hazards and risks are not sufficiently integrated with land use planning.[10] Non-integration of hazard and risk information in urban development planning increases vulnerability to disasters, the impacts of which may be aggravated by the concentration of population and assets in vulnerable locations.

---

[4] World Bank. Databank. World Development Indicators. Arable land (hectares per person) (accessed 23 August 2023).

[5] ADB. 2016. *50 Years of ADB: Improving Lives for a Better Future. Asian Development Bank 2016 Annual Report.* Manila.

[6] Food and Agriculture Organization of the United Nations (FAO), International Fund for Agriculture and Development (IFAD), United Nations Children's Fund (UNICEF), World Food Programme (WFP), and World Health Organization (WHO). 2019. *The State of Food Security and Nutrition in the World 2019. Safeguarding Against Economic Slowdowns and Downturns.* Rome.

[7] Fergana Valley, not shown on Figure 2, lies mainly in eastern Uzbekistan but also extends to southern part of the Kyrgyz Republic and northern Tajikistan.

[8] Ministry of Economic Development and Trade of the Republic of Tajikistan. 2016. *National Development Strategy of the Republic of Tajikistan for the Period Up to 2030.* Dushanbe.

[9] University of Notre Dame. Notre Dame Global Adaptation Initiative (ND-GAIN). Rankings – Tajikistan (accessed 23 August 2023).

[10] Central Asia Regional Economic Cooperation (CAREC) Program. 2022. *Tajikistan Country Risk Profile.*

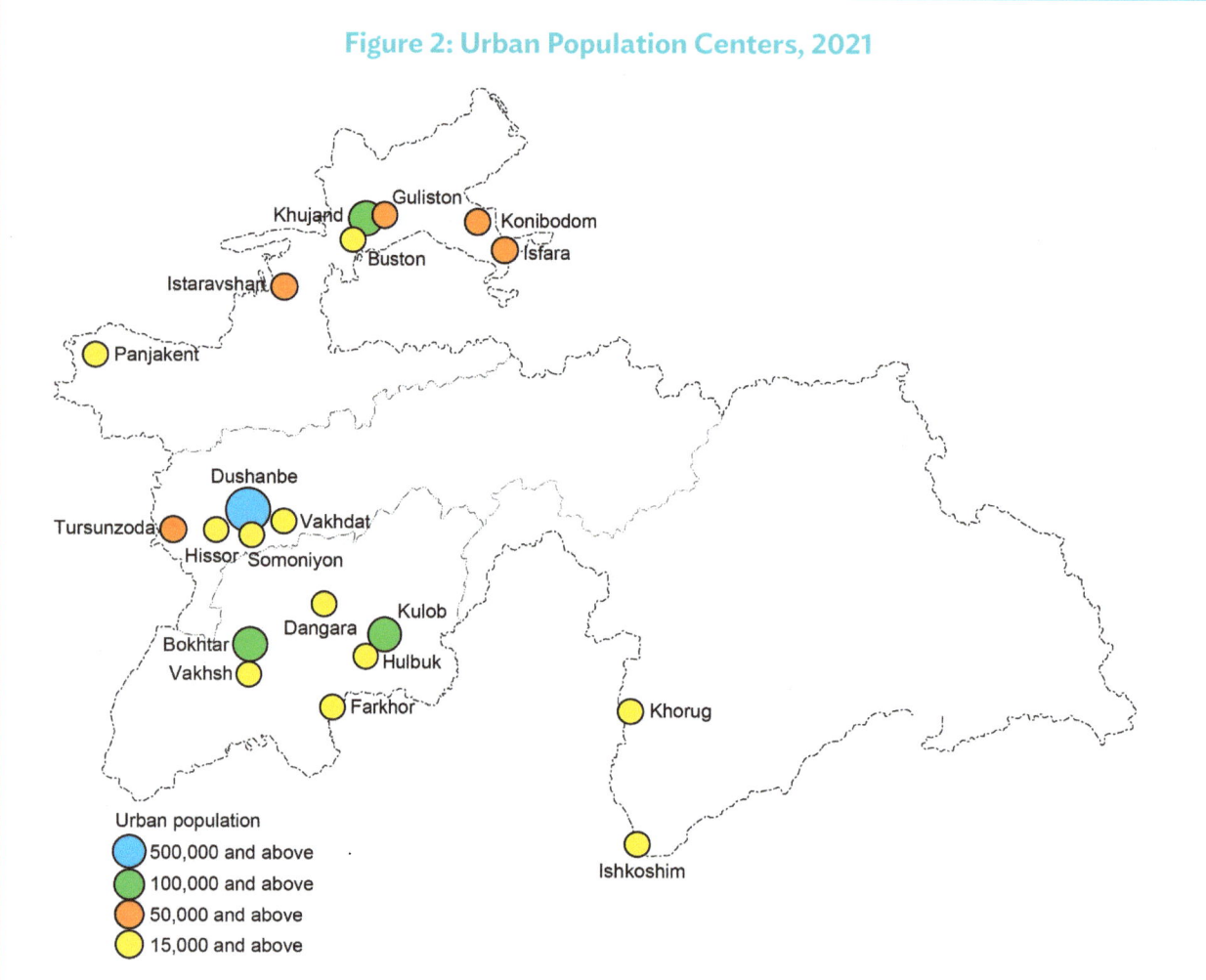

Figure 2: Urban Population Centers, 2021

Note: The names of places in this figure are based on the Asian Development Bank country base map for Tajikistan. Their spelling may differ from the English names used in government documents.

Source: Authors, using Asian Development Bank basemap on Tajikistan and population data from Agency on Statistics under the President of the Republic of Tajikistan. 2021. *Demographic Yearbook of the Republic of Tajikistan, 30th Anniversary of State Independence, 2021* (available in hard copy only).

South Central Asia, including Tajikistan, is an active seismic zone. According to the Global Earthquake Hazard Map, the whole country is in the high to very high-risk zone, and epicenters may be almost everywhere.[11] Strong earthquakes are frequent and represent a substantial threat to cities like Dushanbe, where a potential earthquake magnitude can be as high as 8–9 on the Richter scale, and to reservoir dams where hydropower plants are located.[12] Experts have estimated that earthquakes in Tajikistan affected 70,000 to 100,000 people from 1910 to 2010. The most severe earthquakes, causing hundreds of deaths and significant economic

---

[11] M. Pagani et al. 2018. *Global Earthquake Model (GEM) Seismic Hazard Map* (version 2018.1 - December 2018).

[12] M. Zaripova. 2018. *Tajikistan Disaster Risk Profile*. Emergency and Disaster Reports. 5 (3). University of Oviedo – Department of Medicine. Unit for Research in Emergency and Disaster.

losses, occurred in 1911 and 1946. The last earthquake in Dushanbe, in 1949, resulted in more than 30,000 deaths. The national loss from a 100-year earthquake would total an estimated $885 million. The risk is exacerbated by the scant number of buildings (less than 5%) certified as earthquake resistant.[13]

Temperature rises in Tajikistan are projected to be above the global average, which increases the probability of heat waves and droughts. Over the last 65 years, the average annual temperature has increased by 1.2°C–1.9°C in the cities of Tajikistan.[14] UN estimates suggest that warming could reach 5.5°C by the 2090s, compared with a 1986–2005 baseline.[15] Temperatures are highly likely to more regularly surpass 40°C, particularly in lowland regions. The probability of heat wave conditions is projected to increase dramatically, reaching 7%–23% by the 2090s. Tajikistan ranks eighth in the world in terms of exposure to drought. Models suggest very significant increases in the annual probability of meteorological drought, from 3% to over 25% by the 2050s.

Tajikistan is vulnerable to floods and landslides. Unpredictable weather patterns affect the country's glaciers, which have lost 30% of their area mass over the past 50–60 years. They also increase the risk of sudden floods from glacier lake outburst floods (footnote 12). Projected increases in extreme rainfall intensity and frequency will lead to flash flooding, landslides, and mudslides. The average annual number of people affected by floods is estimated at 29,800, with fatalities averaging 45 (footnote 9). An average of $60.8 million is also estimated to be lost to floods annually, nearly 80% of which is sustained by Khatlon, home to 36% of the country's population and major cities including Bokhtar. About 85% of the country's territory is at risk of mudflows, 75% is vulnerable to avalanches, and nearly 36% is at risk of landslides.[16] Greater climate variability is projected to compound these risks.

Tajikistan updated its nationally determined contributions in 2021. The country enhanced its adaptation and mitigation ambitions to support sustainable and efficient development, taking into consideration its national circumstances. Specifically, it has revised its climate agenda to focus on five national priority sectors: energy, agriculture, forestry and biodiversity, transport and infrastructure, and industry and construction. Furthermore, it has committed to an unconditional contribution of reducing its greenhouse gas emissions by 2030 to 60%–70% of 1990 levels. With financing support from the international community, it proposes a conditional contribution of 10% more emissions reduction.[17] The identified priority sectors and updated commitments align with the national priorities embodied in multiple key national strategies, including the NDS 2016–2030, the National Climate Change Adaptation Strategy 2019–2030, and the Medium-Term Development Program 2021–2025.

---

[13] Government of the Republic of Tajikistan. 2022. *Strategy for the Development of the Construction Industry of the Republic of Tajikistan for the Period Up to 2030*. Resolution Number 203. Dated April 27, 2022 (unofficially translated).

[14] P. Khakimov et al. 2020. Climate Change Effects on Agriculture and Food Security in Tajikistan. *Silk Road: A Journal of Eurasian Development*. 2 (1). pp. 89–112.

[15] World Bank Group and ADB. 2021. *Climate Risk Country Profile: Tajikistan*.

[16] World Bank. Climate Change Knowledge Portal. Tajikistan (accessed 23 August 2023).

[17] Government of the Republic of Tajikistan. 2021. The Updated NDC of the Republic of Tajikistan.

Population Growth and Age Structure

The population is projected to increase at a fast rate over the next 30 years. From the 9.51 million census results it announced in 2021, the Agency on Statistics under the President of the Republic of Tajikistan (TAJSTAT) has projected that the country's population will reach 16.2 million by 2050 and 25.3 million by the end of the century.[18] The fertility rate, relatively high at 3.61 births per woman, helps keep a positive population balance despite migration. The population is young with a median age of 22.4 years. The urban population is projected to increase from 2.5 million to 2.8 million in 2025.[19] In spite of that, the urban-to-rural population ratio is expected to remain at about 27% urban and 73% rural. The low urban proportion can be attributed to the continuing predominant role of agriculture in the economy, the sluggish pace of industrial development, and the insufficient creation of employment in the services sector (footnote 17).

The NDS identifies the demographic dividend as an opportunity to increase urbanization. According to the NDS, the working-age population, which will reach 60% of the total in 15 years, provides an opportunity for economic development (Figure 3).[20] To capitalize on this and avoid a turn to a "window of demographic threat," the NDS acknowledges the need to develop adequate infrastructure and employment opportunities. It specifically highlights the need for "accelerated urbanization," the construction of housing at a large scale, and investments in transport as well as social infrastructure (footnote 19).

Urban and Ethnic Composition

Tajikistan is the least urbanized country in Central Asia in demographic terms. In 2020, the country's urban population was 2.5 million, or 26.2% of the total.[21] This was significantly below the 37% urban population proportion in 1970, which was overall comparable to those of its immediate neighbors (Table 2). Among the reasons for the decrease are deurbanization due to the collapse of the Soviet Union in 1991[22] and the civil war in 1992–1997, which resulted in emigration and socioeconomic crisis,[23] the economic predominance of agriculture (22.6% of GDP), insufficient industrialization (17% of GDP) and urban jobs, lack of affordable housing units and high mortgage rate (22% per annum), in addition to the impact that *propiska*, the mandatory registration of residence, may have on population dynamics. Such impact has yet to be fully analyzed, but no policy change appears imminent.

---

[18] The preliminary 2020 census results also indicated the following increases in regional populations: GBAO–227,200 (206,000 in 2010); Sugd–2,770,000 (2,233,000 in 2010); Khatlon–3,444,000 (2,677,000 in 2010); Dushanbe–948,800 (724,000 in 2010); and DRS–2,270,000 (1,722,000 in 2010).

[19] Government of the Republic of Tajikistan. 2021. Annex to the Decree of the Government of the Republic of Tajikistan. Programme of Medium-Term Development of the Republic of Tajikistan for 2021–2025 (Russian original, excerpted in English by FAO).

[20] The working age in Tajikistan is 15–62 years for men and 15–57 years for women.

[21] Agency on Statistics under the President of the Republic of Tajikistan. Preliminary results of the population and housing census for 2020.

[22] A majority of the Russian-speaking population who emigrated previously lived in urban areas.

[23] Center for Economic Research, United Nations Economic and Social Commission for Asia and the Pacific, and United Nations Development Programme. 2013. Urbanization in Central Asia: Challenges, Issues and Prospects. *Analytical Report 2013/3*. Tashkent: Center for Economic Research.

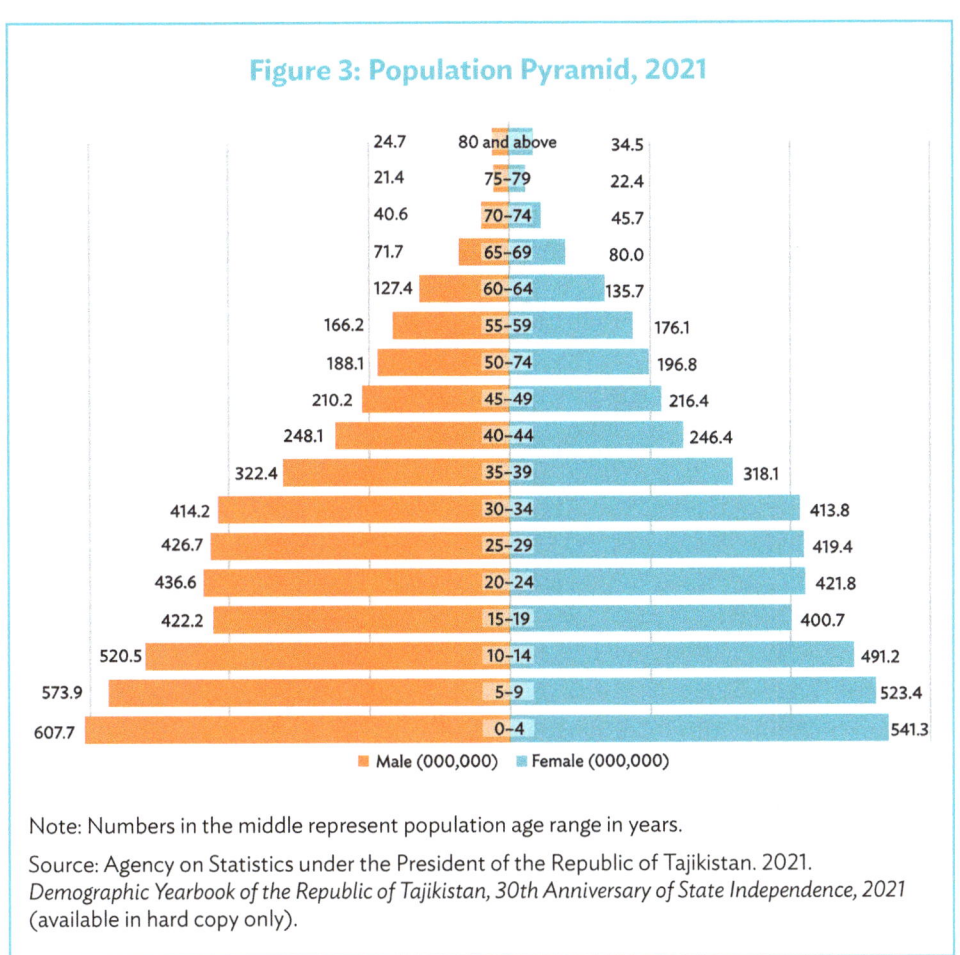

Note: Numbers in the middle represent population age range in years.

Source: Agency on Statistics under the President of the Republic of Tajikistan. 2021. *Demographic Yearbook of the Republic of Tajikistan, 30th Anniversary of State Independence, 2021* (available in hard copy only).

Table 2: Urban Population Proportion of Central Asian Countries, 2000, 2007, and 2020 (% of total)

Country	2000	2007	2020
Uzbekistan	46.0	37.0	50.0
Tajikistan	26.5	37.0	27.5
Kazakhstan	56.0	50.0	58.0
Turkmenistan	46.0	48.0	53.0
Kyrgyz Republic	35.0	37.0	37.0

Source: World Bank. Data. *Urban Population (% of Total Population)* (accessed July 2023).

Tajikistan has an ethnically and culturally diverse population. More than 75% of the population is Tajik, a percentage that has increased with the emigration of non-Tajiks during the civil war of 1992–1997, while 15% are Uzbeks and about 1% are Russians. A predominantly Muslim country (97%), the remainder of the population includes Orthodox Christians and Catholics. Historically, the population has strong cultural ties with Iran, as their languages are closely related and mutually intelligible. The official language of Tajikistan is Tajik, written in Cyrillic characters and belonging to the Persian language group. It is very similar to Farsi, spoken in Iran, and Dari, a language in Afghanistan.[24] Russian is also widely spoken.

Migration

Out-migration from Tajikistan has been significant since its independence in 1991. The 1992–1997 civil war claimed over 50,000 lives, displaced some 1.2 million people, and triggered economic collapse and food and fuel shortages.[25] Political and economic instability, lack of employment opportunities, and low wages led to significant migration.[26] The unstable pre-war climate following the dissolution of the Soviet Union in 1991 was particularly characterized by the emigration of the Russian-speaking population. By 1995, almost half of the Russian-speaking population (42%) had left the country for Russia (presently, known as the Russian Federation), Germany (ethnic Germans), Uzbekistan (ethnic Uzbeks), Kazakhstan (mostly ethnic Russians), and Israel (Jewish repatriates).

Migrants constitute around 12% of the total population. Estimates place the unemployed at almost 55% of Tajikistan's total labor force. Further, unemployment motivated almost 92% of external migration.[27] About 1 million Tajik workers have migrated to foreign countries over the past 10 years. With 57% of the population under the age of 24, and a growing supply of labor market entrants, every third family in the country has at least one member working outside Tajikistan. Migration is especially high from the mountainous regions. Although men make up the bigger chunk, the number of women leaving the country to work abroad has went up from 11% of the total during the mid-2010s to 16% of the total as of the end of 2020.[28] Facilitated by regular air links, visa-free travel, a significant Tajik diaspora community, and language familiarity, the main migration destination, at over 90%, is the Russian Federation. Migration to Kazakhstan accounts for about 4% of the total, while migration to the United Arab Emirates, the Republic of Korea, and Eastern European countries is aggregately less than 1%. Tajik migrant workers are mainly employed in construction (75%), commerce (10%), agriculture (7%), and industry (6%). Most migrants (73%) work outside Tajikistan seasonally, typically from February–March to October–November. In 2016, the provinces of GBAO, Sugd, and Khatlon registered a negative net migration, while the DRS and Dushanbe had a positive net migration.[29]

---

[24] ADB placed on hold its regular assistance in Afghanistan effective 15 August 2021.

[25] United States Agency for International Development (USAID). USAID Country Profile. *Property Rights and Resource Governance: Tajikistan.*

[26] United Nations Economic Commission for Europe (UNECE). 2011. *Country Profiles on the Housing Sector: Tajikistan* (English and Russian).

[27] ADB. 2020. *Strengthening Support for Labor Migration in Tajikistan: Assessment and Recommendations.* Manila.

[28] Integral Human Development. *Country Profiles. Tajikistan.*

[29] TAJSTAT. Regions of Tajikistan Republic, 2017 (in Russian).

1.3 Economy

Tajikistan has made significant progress in growing its economy and reducing poverty. The economy grew at an average rate of 7% per year over the last two decades, and poverty fell from 83% of the population in 2000 to 27.4% in 2018.[30] International migration has been a major driver of this economic advancement, with remittances generating one-third of GDP in 2019 (footnote 27). The economy is predominantly rural, accounting for 22.6% of GDP, while industry contributes 23.6% and services 13.4%.[31] However, per capita GDP in 2022 was the lowest in Central Asia, at $1,054.20.[32]

Sector Analysis

Productivity of agriculture, Tajikistan's main sector, is low. Tajikistan's primary crops are cereals (mainly wheat) and cotton. Cropping patterns have remained the same since the 1990s, although the importance of cereals and legumes has steadily increased, and that of cotton has decreased. Wheat is grown in 35% and fodder in 15% of the total arable cropped area, while cotton is cultivated in 43% of the irrigated area that comprises 30.1% of the total arable land. Agricultural productivity is low compared to other countries in the region. For example, yields of major crops (2.2 tons/ha for wheat, 1.7 tons/ha for cotton, and 21.9 tons/ha for potatoes) are significantly below Uzbekistan's yields (4.5 tons/ha for wheat, 2.3 tons/ha for cotton, and 24.5 tons/ha for potatoes) which are already low by international standards.[33]

Tajikistan's industrial sector is concentrated on a few state-owned enterprises. Tajikistan's major heavy industries are aluminum processing and chemical production. The Tursunzoda Aluminum Smelter, built in 1975, is the third-largest processing plant in the world. Aside from aluminum and other processed metals, the intermediate and heavy industry subsectors produce engineering goods, hydroelectricity, power transformers, cables, and agricultural equipment. Chemical production plants are in Dushanbe, Bokhtar, and Yavan. Tajikistan is the world's third-largest producer of hydroelectric power, behind the United States and the Russian Federation. About 85% of Tajikistan's current hydroelectric power is produced by stations along the Vakhsh River. Production, transportation, and distribution of electricity are under the state-owned joint-stock company, Barqi Tojik. Light industries are mainly in textiles and food, processing domestically harvested fruit, wheat, tobacco, and other agricultural products, as well as ginning and the sale of cotton fiber.

---

[30] World Bank. Data. GDP Growth (Annual %) – Tajikistan (accessed July 2023) and World Bank. *The World Bank in Tajikistan*.
[31] USAID. *Tajikistan Economic Growth and Trade*.
[32] World Bank. Data. GDP Per Capita (Current US$) – Europe & Central Asia (accessed 30 October 2023).
[33] Sector Assessment (Summary): Agriculture and Natural Resources. In ADB. 2016. *Tajikistan: Country Partnership Strategy (2016–2020)*. Manila.

Construction is one of the key industries for growth. Construction's share of the country's GDP was around 16% in 2020 and expected to reach 19.5% by 2030 (footnote 13). This is a remarkable contribution when compared with neighboring Uzbekistan where the contribution of construction was estimated by an Asian Development Bank (ADB) study at 6.5% in 2019.[34] According to the Strategy for the Development of the Construction Industry, the average annual employment in construction, which in 2020 was around 109,000, will increase by 20% in 10 years. To support this, the government plans to improve the investment environment for foreign and domestic investors and introduce public–private partnership (PPP) mechanisms.

Remittances in Tajikistan constitute over a third of GDP. Remittances play a significant role in the economic and social stability of many Tajik families. In 2017, $2.2 billion was remitted, accounting for 37% of the GDP.[35] In absolute terms, around $34.3 billion was remitted to Tajikistan during 2002–2018, which is about $500 per capita per annum. Remittances are mostly spent on consumer and household goods, 57% of which, on average, are spent on immediate consumption needs.[36] This suggests that many of the recipients heavily depend on remittances and are prone to income insecurity.

Tajikistan is in the early stage of transitioning from a planned to market economy. Over the past century, several factors isolated Tajikistan both economically and socially. As part of the former Soviet Union, the country was subsidy-dependent, and production facilities, trade, transport, and energy were centrally planned from Moscow. Following independence, the dissolution of a unified economic area in post-Soviet Central Asia and the lack of trade with neighbors have constrained economic progress. The situation was exacerbated by the 1992–1997 civil war, which delayed legal and institutional reforms. Since the end of the war, the state has passed a series of laws, presidential decrees, and regulations promoting private property and land reform, but land use and ownership continue to be restrictive (footnote 25). A favorable context for opening up has developed with the reopening of border crossings and visa waivers with Uzbekistan after two decades of blockade.

Coronavirus Disease and Post-Pandemic Outlook

The impact of the coronavirus disease (COVID-19) pandemic on lives and the health system was unprecedented in Tajikistan's post-civil war history. The pandemic hit when the economy and livelihoods were already fragile following several economic disruptions in the past decade. The economic implications of the COVID-19 outbreak became apparent soon after the first cases.[37] The closure of borders with neighboring countries, including main trading partners, disrupted trade and transport ties and slowed the implementation of investment projects. Restrictions on labor mobility and economic activity at home and abroad led to a decline in remittances by migrants and a drop in consumer demand and investment. Currently, Tajikistan is entering the post-recovery phase.

---

[34] ADB. 2021. *Harnessing Uzbekistan's Potential of Urbanization: National Urban Assessment.* Manila.
[35] World Bank. World Development Indicators.
[36] International Labour Organization. 2010. *Migrant Remittances to Tajikistan.* Geneva.
[37] The first cases were officially declared in May 2020.

Opening up is required to attract investment. Large capital inflows are needed to finance flagship infrastructure projects, e.g., the Rogun hydropower plant and the modernization of the Tursunzoda aluminum plant. Tajikistan managed to secure investments from the PRC and international financing institutions (IFIs) and successfully issued Eurobonds in 2017. With 47.3% of foreign investments, the PRC is the most important foreign investor in Tajikistan, followed by the Russian Federation (31.3%) and Switzerland (6.8%).[38] The PRC and Tajikistan have maintained regular high-level contacts and cooperation since border issues were settled and diplomatic ties were established.

The relationship between Tajikistan and Uzbekistan is improving. Between 1991 and 2018, relations with Uzbekistan were tense, but they have significantly improved since the state visit of Uzbek President Mirziyoyev in March 2018 when accords were signed in trade, economy, investment, finance, transport, agriculture, water and energy, taxes, customs, tourism, education and science, health, culture, interregional cooperation, and security and countering crime. However, the relationship with the Kyrgyz Republic remains strained due to armed border conflicts in May 2021 and September 2022.

Private Sector

Private sector activity is constrained by weak governance, an unclear regulatory environment, corruption, high transport costs, erratic electricity supply, foreign exchange shortages, and limited access to long-term financing. According to the NDS, private investment's share of GDP was 5% in 2015, significantly below the 21% average in the Commonwealth of Independent States.[39] Business creation rates are over 10 times lower than in the Kyrgyz Republic and Kazakhstan.[40] Jobs in the private sector[41] represent 11%–13% of total employment and are concentrated in agriculture, trade, hospitality, and manufacturing.[42] A report from the World Bank concluded that building an enabling environment for private sector development requires decisive governance reforms designed to reduce the role of the state (footnote 39).

Individual entrepreneurs account for most registered businesses. Only 10% of over 300,000 active small and medium-sized enterprises in Tajikistan are registered as firms or companies. The remaining 90% are registered as individual entrepreneurs classified as (i) patent-holders (a form of business registration allowing owners

---

[38] World Bank. Macroeconomics & Fiscal Management Global Practice. 2017. Heightened Vulnerabilities Despite Sustained Growth. *Tajikistan Country Economic Update*. Fall 2017.

[39] World Bank. 2018. *Tajikistan Systematic Country Diagnostic: Making the National Development Strategy 2030 a Success – Building the Foundation for Shared Prosperity*. Washington, DC.

[40] In Tajikistan, only 1.8 companies are created annually on average for every 10,000 working-age persons, against 13 in the Kyrgyz Republic and 22 in Kazakhstan.

[41] The official definition of the private sector includes enterprises with less than 50% state participation.

[42] International Development Association. Finance, Competitiveness and Innovation Global Practice Europe and Central Asia Region. 2019. Project Appraisal Document on a Proposed Grant to the Republic of Tajikistan for a Rural Economy Development Project. Washington, DC.

to operate under a simplified tax arrangement), (ii) certificate holders, and (iii) *dehkan* farmers (privately owned farms established after the dissolution of Soviet-era state and collective farms). *Dehkan* farmers account for 61% of all individual entrepreneurs.[43]

1.4 Political History and System of Governance

Tajikistan is a unitary republic with a dominant party system. The Constitution was adopted in 1994 and amended in 1999, 2003, and 2016. Presidential elections are held every 7 years, and Parliament elections every 5 years. It is, however, a presidential republic with a one-party dominant system, where the President's People's Democratic Party of Tajikistan routinely has a vast majority in Parliament. Article 69 of the Constitution of the Republic of Tajikistan empowers the President to appoint and dismiss the chairpersons of the subnational governments of GBAO, the regions, Dushanbe, and the towns and districts. The appointments and dismissals are submitted to the Parliament for confirmation. The administrative and territorial divisions, in terms of number and their permanent (*propiska*-registered) populations, are shown below (Table 3).

Table 3: Administrative and Territorial Divisions

	Area (1,000 km²)	Permanent Population (1,000s)	Number of				
			Districts	Cities	Districts within Cities	Towns	Rural *Jamoats*
Tajikistan	141.4	9,506.3	62	18	4	65	368
Dushanbe	0.1	880.8	0	1	4	0	0
GBAO	62.9	231.4	7	1	0	4	42
Sugd	25.2	2,753.1	14	8	0	23	93
Khatlon	24.7	3,425.5	24	4	0	23	132
DRS	28.5	2,215.5	13	4	0	15	101

DRS = Districts of Republican Subordination, GBAO = Gorno-Badakhshan Autonomous *Oblast* (Mountainous Badakhshan Autonomous Region), km² = square kilometers.

Source: Agency on Statistics under the President of the Republic of Tajikistan. 2021. *Demographic Yearbook of the Republic of Tajikistan, 30th Anniversary of State Independence, 2021* (available in hard copy only).

In territorial terms, there is a strong vertical hierarchy of power, and decentralization is not high on the policy agenda. The subnational government (SNG) structure in Tajikistan has three tiers (Figure 4). The first tier consists of the *oblasts* (regions) of GBAO, Sugd, and Khatlon. The second tier is made up of *rayons* (districts) and cities closely resembling municipalities. In total, there are 62 districts in

---

[43] Tajikistan Tax Committee under the Government of the Republic of Tajikistan (information available only in hard copy Russian document).

Tajikistan: GBAO, Sugd, and Khatlon have 45 districts, the DRS has 13, and Dushanbe has four. The *jamoats*, which are like communities, comprise the lowest SNG tier. As of January 2020, Tajikistan has more than 400 *jamoats*, 368 of which are rural.[44] Appointment and dismissal of the chairpersons of the first and second tiers are by the president, while the *rayon* heads appoint and dismiss the chairpersons of *jamoats*. The executive bodies of state authority in *oblasts* and *rayons* are *hukumats*.

Jamoats, as well as regions and districts, are formed on a territorial basis and possess a legal status and an official seal. Municipal property may include means of transportation, equipment, and other facilities, either state- or community-owned, which local governments have built, purchased, or acquired ownership of through transfer, etc. Town or village revenue sources include budget allocations from city or district councils and voluntary donations of citizens and working collectives.[45] Other than these, there are no legal mechanisms for towns and villages to generate their own revenues.

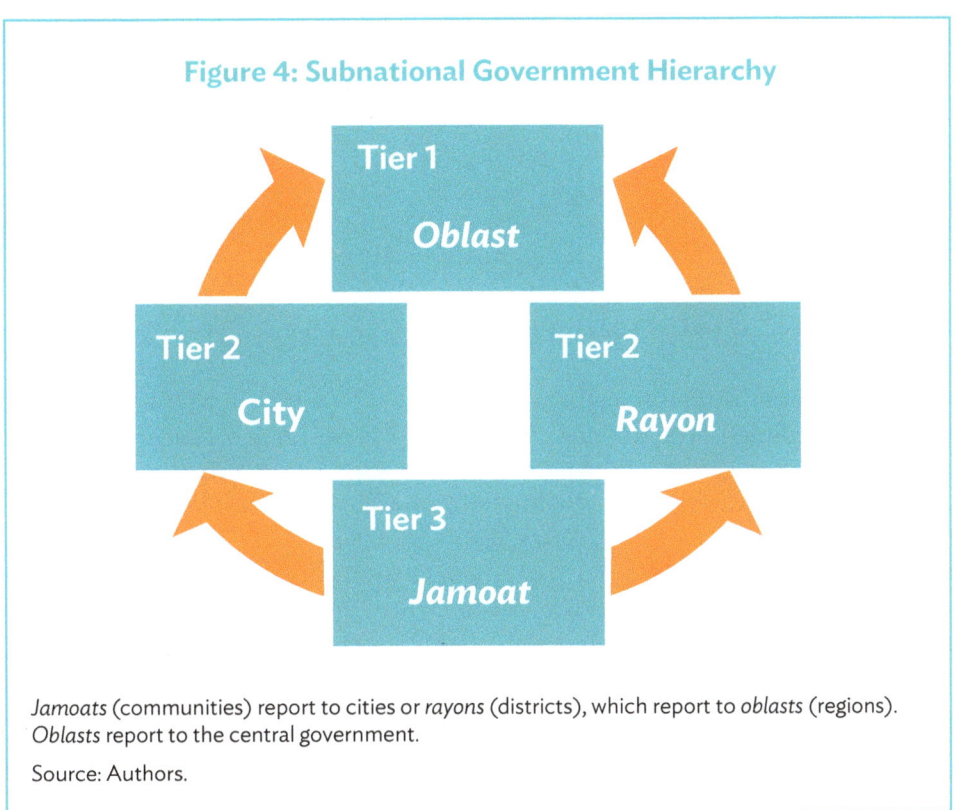

Figure 4: Subnational Government Hierarchy

Jamoats (communities) report to cities or *rayons* (districts), which report to *oblasts* (regions). *Oblasts* report to the central government.

Source: Authors.

---

[44] TAJSTAT. *Population of the Republic of Tajikistan as of 1 January 2020 Report* (available in hard copy only).

[45] Law of the Republic of Tajikistan "On Local Self-government in Towns and Villages."

Urban Profile

2.1 Urbanization Trends

About a quarter of Tajikistan's population lives in cities. In 2020, the urban population was 2.5 million, or 26.2% of the total, making Tajikistan the least urbanized country in Central Asia (footnote 18). The urban proportion of the country's population has remained broadly constant at this level for the past two decades. Between 2000 and 2013, it stayed at around 26.5%, and in 2013, started to increase slowly, but rising only by 1.5% more until 2020.[46]

Estimates indicate that the urban population could more than double by 2050. Between 2000 and 2021, Tajikistan's population grew by about 53%, from 6.2 million to 9.5 million, while the urban population grew by about 53.5%, from 1.6 million to 2.5 million. A UN regional agency forecasted that the country will undergo a period of rapid urbanization, with the urban population proportion increasing from 27.5% in 2020 to 43% by 2050.[47] With the total population forecast at 16 million, the number of urban dwellers will swell to 6.8 million. This will more than double the present urban population.

The *propiska* system of residence registration is mandatory but its impact on urbanization is unclear. The registration of an individual at the place of residence, known as *propiska*, is mandatory for citizens to have access to social benefits such as housing, employment, health, kindergarten, and school.[48] To submit an application there is a long list of required documents that must be presented within 15 days after settling in the place of residence.[49] There are two types of *propiska*, permanent and temporary (from 3 months to 1 year for students and workers). To obtain a permanent *propiska*, applicants need to own a house or be included in the household registered by the owner of the property. Because living in a city without being registered is administratively punishable, this may be considered a deterrent to urban migration; however, no complete analysis of this has yet been made. Nevertheless, many people are estimated to live and work in cities without

---

[46] World Bank. Data. Urban Population (% of Total Population) – Tajikistan (accessed 23 August 2023).
[47] United Nations Economic and Social Commission for Asia and the Pacific. 2020. *Urbanization and Resource Trends in Tajikistan.*
[48] X. Mironova. 2021. Loss of Harmony: The Rise of a New Tajikistan and the Fall of Old Aspirations for the Better. *The Foreign Policy Centre.* 17 May.
[49] Government Resolution of the Republic of Tajikistan. 2014. Rules for Issuing a Passport of a Citizen of the Republic of Tajikistan, §5. Registration and Discharge, 2014.

propiska; in Dushanbe, some 500,000 people or more are believed to lack one.[50] This means that Dushanbe could have around 1.3 million–1.5 million inhabitants.[51] Through *propiska*, the government maintains control over the population's location and domestic migration and commands citizens over obligations such as payment of taxes, fines, alimonies, and military service.[52] *Propiska* remains a sensitive issue and its relaxation does not appear to be on the government's agenda.

2.2 Urban Hierarchy and Settlement Types

Over half of the urban population is concentrated in Dushanbe, Khujand, Bokhtar, and Kulob. The capital, Dushanbe, is Tajikistan's largest and most important city.[53] With 916,000 official inhabitants in 2022, it is home to at least 35.2% of the country's urban population.[54] In 2021, Dushanbe together with the next three major cities of Khujand, Kulob, and Bokhtar accounted for more than half of the country's urban population (Table 4). Khujand is a regional hub due to its geographic location.

Table 4: Urban Population
(as of 1 January 2021)

City	Population
Dushanbe	880,800
Khujand	185,500
Kulob	107,700
Bokhtar	113,400
Istaravshan	66,400
Konibodom	52,800
Qayroqqum	50,000
Vahdat	44,100
Isfara	52,700
Tursunzoda	57,100

Source: Agency on Statistics under the President of the Republic of Tajikistan. 2021. *Demographic Yearbook of the Republic of Tajikistan, 30th Anniversary of State Independence, 2021* (available in hard copy only).

---

[50] Estimate based on consultations with key stakeholders.
[51] Consultation with the Institute of Economics and Demography of the Academy of Sciences of Tajikistan.
[52] Republic of Tajikistan. Code of Administrative Offenses (Violations) of the Republic of Tajikistan. Article 469 (in Russian).
[53] With more than 500,000 people, according to the Urban Planning Code.
[54] Sector Assessment (Summary): Water and Other Urban Infrastructure and Services (Urban Water Supply and Sanitation). In ADB. 2022. *Report and Recommendation of the President: Additional Financing for Dushanbe Water Supply and Sanitation*. Manila.

Most cities are medium or small. The 2016 Urban Planning Code (amended 2020) has classified the country's settlements into urban (cities and towns) and rural, although no strict delineation by population size has been made between small cities, towns, and rural settlements. Under the code, small cities and towns have fewer than 50,000 inhabitants, while some villages have more than 5,000 inhabitants.[55] Cities with 50,000–100,000 inhabitants have been classified as intermediate. However, the Agency on Statistics, TAJSTAT, has used a different classification system when reporting on the urban population. Specifically, it uses a population size of below 10,000 to refer to small cities and towns and categorizes intermediate cities as either medium or big cities and towns, with the population of medium cities and towns ranging from 10,000 to 40,000 and big cities and towns ranging from 40,000 to 100,000. Therefore, it has reported no small cities and indicated medium-sized cities and towns as the biggest category of urban settlements in Tajikistan as of 2021 (Table 5). In contrast, under the Urban Planning Code's classification system, 11 small cities have been identified, comprising more than half the total number of cities and about 37% of the urban population.[56] Of the 16 cities monitored by TAJSTAT, nine grew rapidly at over 2% per year in 2000–2021 (Table 6).

Table 5: Classification and Population of Urban Settlements
(as of 1 January 2021)

Size: Number of Inhabitants	Number of Urban Settlements		Combined Population (100,000)		Share in Total Urban Population (%)		
	Cities	Towns	Cities	Towns	Cities	Towns	Both
Large: >100,000	4	0	1,287.4	0	51.5	0	51.5
Big: 40,000–100,000	6	0	316.9	0	12.7	0	12.7
Medium: 10,000–40,000	8	33	167.5	597.9	6.7	23.9	30.6
Small: <10,000	0	28	0	132.1	0	5.3	5.3
Subtotal	18	61	1,771.8	730.0	70.8	29.2	100.0
Total	79		2,501.8		100.0		

> = greater than, < = less than, TAJSTAT = Agency on Statistics under the President of the Republic of Tajikistan.

Source: Agency on Statistics under the President of the Republic of Tajikistan. 2021. *Demographic Yearbook of the Republic of Tajikistan, 30th Anniversary of State Independence, 2021* (available in hard copy only).

---

[55] This publication refers to the following terms in its usage of city, town, and village: *shahr* = city; *shahrak* = town; and *kishlok* = village.

[56] Like TAJSTAT, the Urban Planning Code has counted 18 cities in Tajikistan. But it has indicated fewer towns (57) and placed the number of villages at 3,950.

Table 6: Urban Population Growth, 2000–2021

City Classification[a]	Total Growth (%)	Average Annual Growth Rate (%)
Dushanbe (large)	55	2.75
Khujand (large)	26	1.30
Kulob (large)	38	1.90
Bokhtar (large)	87	4.35
Istaravshan (big)	31	1.55
Qayroqqum (big)	41	2.05
Vahdat (big)	39	1.95
Isfara (big)	43	2.15
Tursunzoda (big)	51	2.55
Rogun (medium)	92	4.60
Levakant (medium)	68	3.40
Norak (medium)	66	3.30
Istiqlol (medium)	47	2.35
Buston (medium)	40	2.00
Panjakent (medium)	34	1.70
Khorog (medium)	11	0.55

[a] Follows the Agency on Statistics' definition of a large, big, and medium city.

Source: Agency on Statistics under the President of the Republic of Tajikistan. 2021. *Demographic Yearbook of the Republic of Tajikistan, 30th Anniversary of State Independence, 2021* (available in hard copy only).

The classification of cities lacks coherent statistical support. The discrepancy between the city classification system set by the Urban Planning Code and that used by TAJSTAT creates confusion, which could lead to challenges in the implementation and the continued enhancement of the urbanization policy. Particularly, because as a key statistical agency, TAJSTAT is mandated not just to monitor, evaluate, and report on the status of policy execution but also to provide recommendations on making the policies work. This means it needs to ensure that the substance and processes of its statistical systems align with and support the performance of these functions. In this case, it should be able to reflect and advance the goals of the urbanization policy embedded in the Urban Planning Code, and where discrepancies exist, take a proactive role in resolving the discrepancies.

Population growth in Khujand is taking place mainly in peri-urban areas. Buston, Gafurov, and Guliston are municipalities adjacent to Khujand that are not part of its administrative area but share its labor market. Overall, the population of the Khujand agglomeration increased by about 17% in 2010–2020, and most of this is attributable to the growth of peri-urban areas. A desk estimation of the size of the agglomeration (including cities accessible within one hour) indicates that it has about 554,000 inhabitants, an area of 285 square kilometers (km^2), and a population density of 644 inhabitants per km^2 (Table 7).

Table 7: Desk Estimation of the Population in Khujand Agglomeration

Municipality	Population
Khistevarz	83,000
Istaravshan	66,400
Konibodom	52,800
Isfisor	44,600
Buston	37,400
Kurkat	31,000
Ovchi Kalacha	22,000
Gafurov	20,900
Samgar	20,000
Navkat	18,900
Guliston	18,400
Devashtich	18,400
Istiqlol	18,000
Okteppa	18,000
Mekhrobod	16,900
Buston	15,900
Somoniyon	15,700
Dehmoy	14,800
Adrasmon	8,900
Chorukh-Dayron	3,800
Syr Darya	2,900
Palos	2,800
Zarafshon	2,500
Total	**554,000**

Source: Authors, using Google Maps distance calculations and population data from the Agency on Statistics under the President of the Republic of Tajikistan. 2021. *Demographic Yearbook of the Republic of Tajikistan, 30th Anniversary of State Independence, 2021* (available in hard copy only).

There is no agglomeration approach to urbanization in Tajikistan. An agglomeration is not considered a statistical unit and there are no official agglomeration-level data. However, agglomerations are growing particularly fast in Khujand (Figure 5) and Dushanbe. The Dushanbe agglomeration is estimated to have 1,565,000 inhabitants over about 1,685 km², yielding a population density of around 982 inhabitants per km².[57] The estimation considers the municipal administrative area of Dushanbe and the Rudaki, Hissor, Tursunzoda, Yavan, Faizabad, Vahdat, Shahrinav, and Varzob municipalities.

---

[57] TAJSTAT. 2021. Population Number of the Republic of Tajikistan as of 1 January 2021. Agency on Statistics under the President of the Republic of Tajikistan. Dushanbe. The authors utilized geographic information system tools to estimate an agglomeration area encompassing cities and towns within a one-hour radius from Dushanbe.

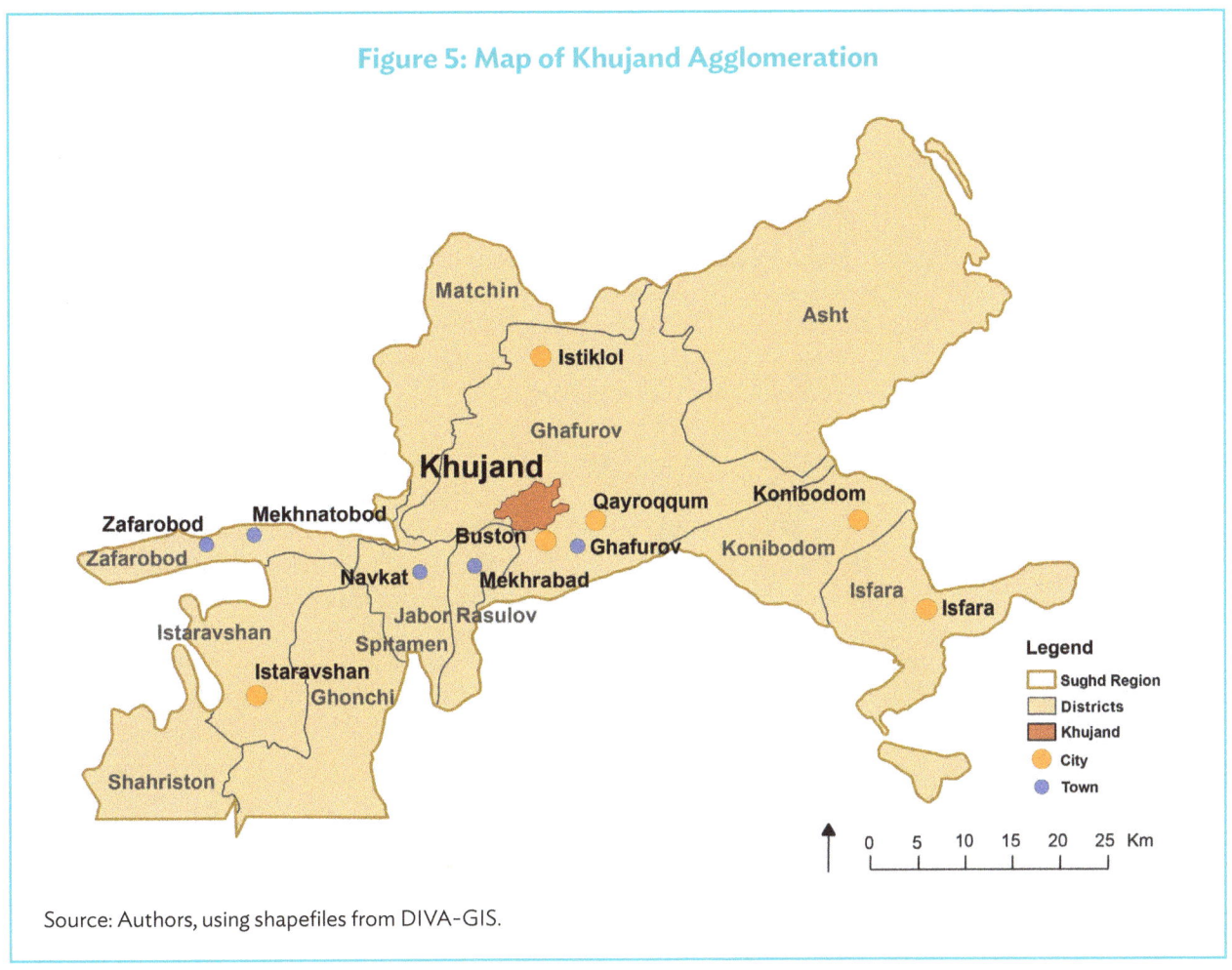

Figure 5: Map of Khujand Agglomeration

Source: Authors, using shapefiles from DIVA-GIS.

2.3 Contribution of Cities to the National Economy

The five largest cities generate around 25% of GDP. In 2020, Dushanbe contributed $1.37 billion or 13% to GDP. The city derives its income mainly from services (including transport and trade), which account for 77.5% of its economic activity.[58] In 2017, Khujand contributed about $400 million or 5% to GDP.[59] The city is industrially developed, with key activities in cotton processing, food production, food canning, and construction materials manufacturing. It received state support

---

[58] Consultations with the executive body of the state authority in Dushanbe and brief analysis of the socioeconomic development of Dushanbe city.

[59] Consultations with the executive body of the state authority in Khujand (unofficial translation of Russian agency name).

in the past for textile and clothing export production.[60] Bokhtar contributes around 4% to GDP,[61] while Kulob generates 2%, 41.5% of which in 2022 came from trade, 30.6% from agriculture, 15.3% from industry, and 12.6% from services.[62] Tursunzoda accounts for 3% of GDP.[63] Aluminum production and processing, led by the Tajik Aluminum Company, considered the largest manufacturing plant in Central Asia, comprises 67.8% of the city's industrial activities.[64]

Small industrial towns make a high contribution to GDP. The industries of Guliston and Panjakent, mainly ore mining and refinery, produced almost half of the total industrial output of the Sugd region in 2016, equivalent to 6% of the total GDP. Similarly, Norak and Yavan accounted for half of the industrial output of the Khatlon region, equivalent to 4% of the total GDP.

Agglomerations: Economic Functions and Comparative Advantages

Dushanbe plays a central administrative, institutional, and service role at the country level. According to the city master plan, Dushanbe's population is expected to grow to 1.05 million by 2040, although the current growth rate suggests this forecast will be significantly exceeded (footnote 53). Unofficial estimates predict that the population by that time will be 1.3–1.5 million (footnote 51). Dushanbe has four administrative districts: Shohmansur, Ismoili Somoni, Firdavsi, and Sino. It serves as a labor, commercial, and administrative center for several cities and rural areas in the DRS. Although cities such as Tursunzoda, Norak, Vahdat, Hissar, and Rogun are functional urban areas with their own industrial activity and labor market, they are gravitating toward Dushanbe due to its proximity and powerful economic activity. Access to Dushanbe from this area of influence is facilitated by a developed road infrastructure. The city also has a good railway connection with neighboring countries like Turkmenistan, Uzbekistan, Kazakhstan, and the Russian Federation. However, the connection to the Kyrgyz Republic and the PRC is still not developed.

Khujand is the economic center of the north and a potential transnational transport hub. The recently proposed Shymkent–Tashkent–Khujand Economic Corridor (STKEC) is expected to expand the trading activities of Khujand and the broader Sugd region with Central Asian countries.[65] Sugd region already accounts for half of the total merchandise exports and imports of Tajikistan. The smaller cities in Khujand's agglomeration need to diversify from the currently dominant agricultural and cotton processing industries.

---

[60] *Asia-Plus*. 2022. Tajikistan Takes Efforts to Improve the International Competitiveness of the Textile and Clothing Sector. 15 March.

[61] Consultations with the executive body of the state authority in Bokhtar (unofficial translation of Russian agency name).

[62] Ministry of Economic Development and Trade of the Republic of Tajikistan (accessed 24 May 2022).

[63] Executive body of the state authority in Tursunzoda (unofficial translation of Russian agency name).

[64] Executive body of the state authority in Tursunzoda. *Tursunzoda City Social and Economic Development Program for 2020–2025*. Available only in Tajik language.

[65] ADB. 2020. *Assessing the Potential of Trade Along the Proposed Shymkent–Tashkent–Khujand Economic Corridor*. Manila.

Bokhtar and Kulob's populations are growing on the back of increasing industrial activity. Petroleum and gas factories have recently opened in Bokhtar and Kulob in the Khatlon region, causing an influx of people into these areas.[66] Cities around Bokhtar, such as Levakand and Kushoniyon, have also grown, with agriculture, cotton production, and construction material production as their main economic activities. Kulob, for its part, has strong tourism potential due to its heritage sites.

Emerging Urban Clusters, Growth Corridors, and Investment Areas

The NDS 2030 identifies urbanization as a regional development priority. Consistent with accelerating urbanization, addressing the connectivity deadlock, and industrializing rapidly, the NDS proposes the development of a system of medium and small towns and large urban settlements as growth poles to enable the growth of corridors and economic activity clusters between them.[67] The system will require coordinated economic development and spatial planning at the regional and local level, and delivery of enabling infrastructure and facilities for production. One of the strategic objectives of NDS is to transform Tajikistan into a transport hub, by improving transport infrastructure, developing corridors, logistics centers, and border terminals, and enhancing interregional and intra-regional connectivity through multimodal development (footnote 8). Freight turnover is expected to double by 2030. The medium-term development programs for 2016–2020 and 2021-2025 have prioritized developing transport corridors (roads, railways, and air) and their associated infrastructure linking to different countries. This has entailed overcoming critical problems such as the poor condition of the road network, limited railway connectivity, insufficient air services, and the absence of logistics centers throughout Tajikistan.

Corridor development has been the dominant approach to strengthening trade and economic cooperation and development. The STKEC is an emerging corridor that will connect and maximize the benefits of the existing Central Asia Regional Economic Cooperation (CAREC) corridors (Figure 6). In 2021, an assessment of the trade potential and a road map for STKEC development were prepared and endorsed by the governments of Kazakhstan, Uzbekistan, and Tajikistan. The transport corridor and associated road networks will support the development of free economic zones in Sugd, Dangara, Panj, and Ishkoshim.[68] Transport corridors with the PRC, India, Iran, and Southeast Asia are less developed, and the rail and road infrastructure in southwest Tajikistan requires significant improvement. In southeast Tajikistan, toward Afghanistan, Pakistan, and India, the development of a corridor to the free economic zone of Panji Poyon will improve trade turnover in Khatlon.[69] The corridor is planned to establish access to Indian seaports.

---

[66] The urban population of Kulob grew by 25% and Bokhtar by 50% from 2000 to 2021. Source: TAJSTAT. Population Number of the Republic of Tajikistan for 2000 and 2021 (unofficially translated).

[67] According to the NDS, these include areas of new industrialization and integration, free trade zones, business incubators, and technological parks.

[68] The importance of free economic zones is discussed in Ministry of Transport of Tajikistan Republic. 2011. State Target Programme for the Development of the Transport Complex in Republic of Tajikistan until 2025. Information can also be found in: The Embassy of the Republic of Tajikistan in the Federal Republic of Germany. 2020. Free economic zones in the Republic of Tajikistan.

[69] Annex to the Decree of the Government of the Republic of Tajikistan. 2021. Programme of Medium-Term Development of the Republic of Tajikistan for 2021–2025 (available in Russian).

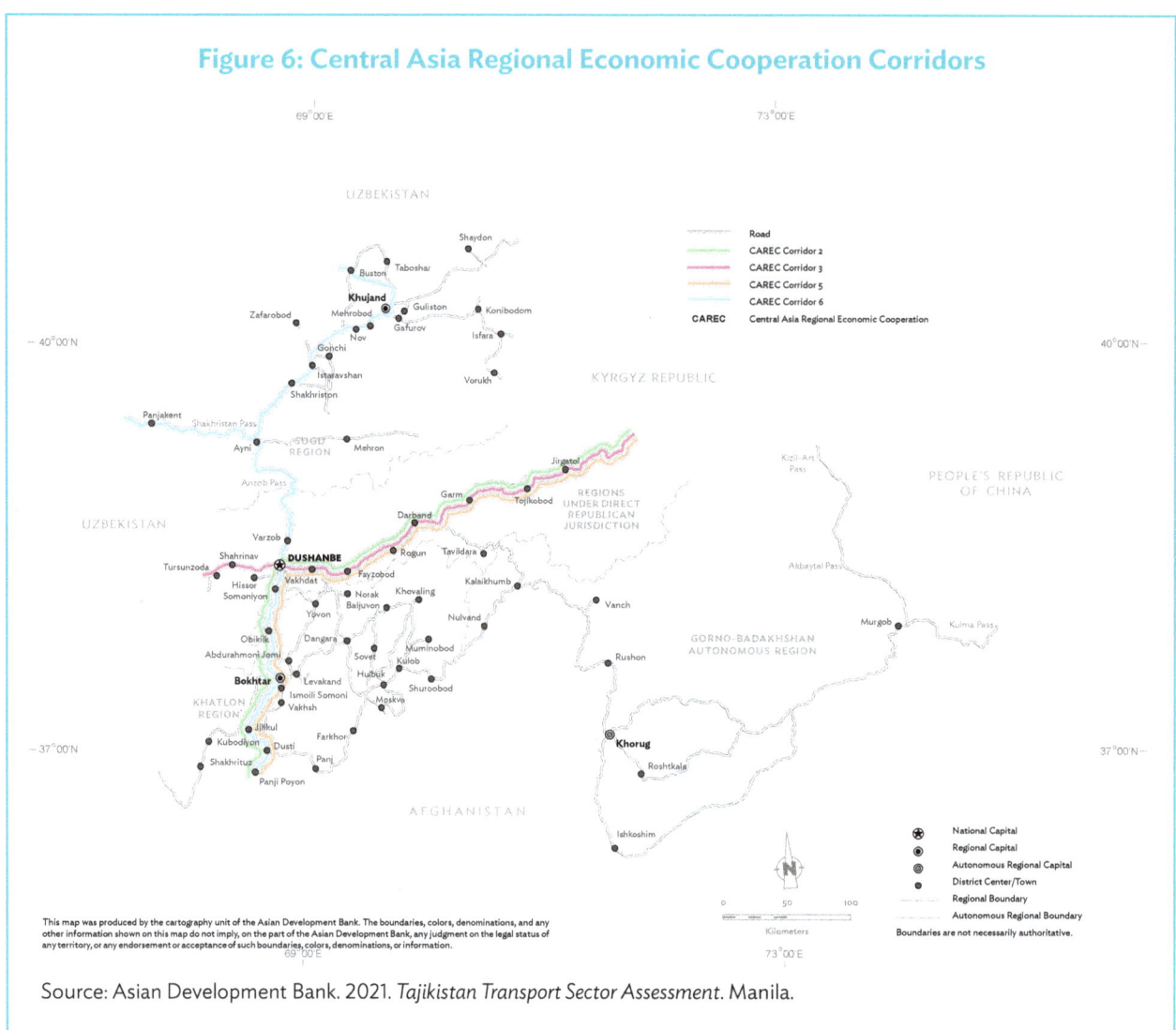

Figure 6: Central Asia Regional Economic Cooperation Corridors

Source: Asian Development Bank. 2021. *Tajikistan Transport Sector Assessment*. Manila.

A cluster approach to economic and spatial development remains to be systematically developed. The NDS identifies energy, agriculture, light industry, tourism, transport, and construction as priority industries. Developing a detailed spatial approach is required to identify target spatial areas and economic activity pairings. An important economic sector is cotton processing and textiles production, which started to be developed in 2006 and clustered in Khujand, Dushanbe, and Bokhtar.[70] Agro-industries and food production facilities are scattered in many cities of Tajikistan, with favorable conditions for a more systematic approach in Khujand and cities in Khatlon and the DRS.[71] Construction materials constitute about

---

[70] Cotton Fiber Processing Program (2007–2015) and Light Industry Development Program (2006–2015), mentioned in ADB. 2010. *Republic of Tajikistan: Implementation Support for Private Sector Development Strategy in Tajikistan*. Consultant's report. Manila. p. 17.

[71] Decree of the Government of the Republic of Tajikistan. On the Concept of Creation and Development of Agro-Industrial Clusters in the Republic of Tajikistan for the Period up to 2040 (available in Russian).

8.4% of the total volume of industrial production in 2019.[72] Factories are located primarily in Sugd (Khujand, Isfara, Jabbor Rasulov, and Gafurov) in proximity to resources. There are existing chemical and petrochemical industries, capitalizing on the availability of raw materials, water, and energy resources in Istiqlol, Isfara, and Guliston in Sugd; and in Yavan and Sarband in Khatlon.

Historic and natural assets make tourism a potential economic sector in Tajikistan. Tajikistan has considerable potential to develop tourism, given its beautiful mountainous landscape, natural assets, and cultural and historical links to the ancient Silk Road routes and even earlier eras.[73] Several cities enjoy thousands of years of history and archeological and cultural monuments of outstanding value. In the last few years, sites along the Great Silk Road have become well-known tourist destinations. The main cities with heritage sites are Hissor, Khujand, and Panjakent as are Kulob and Bokhtar for their religious historical monuments. However, such potential remains largely untapped for various reasons, including poor connectivity, inadequate infrastructure, the lack of a comprehensive tourism ecosystem to ensure quality service delivery, weak institutional and regulatory capacity, and a poor business environment. Tourism requires effective destination promotion and management which is connected to spatial development. The government adopted its National Development Strategy for Tourism in August 2018.[74] The strategy identifies a range of tourism categories (e.g., ecotourism, extreme, mountain, religious, health, historical, cultural, and hunting) but does not strategically prioritize these categories, identify investment needs, or adopt financing plans.[75]

2.4 Spatial Analysis at the Urban Level

Cities in Tajikistan are growing mainly in low-density patterns with single-family houses. Multifamily units constitute only 20% of the total housing stock. The unmet housing demand has compelled home seekers to self-build either authorized or unauthorized single-family houses, which account for about 80% of the stock. Units are built mostly in peri-urban areas that often do not have access to public transport, creating urban sprawl. A sprawl pattern has negative consequences in terms of the high transformation of arable land into built-up areas, the increased cost of providing infrastructure and services to vast extensions which municipalities cannot afford both in terms of capital and operating expenditures, the cost of mobility, and loss of opportunity in long commutes for residents, as well as increased congestion and air pollution.

---

[72] Committee on Architecture and Construction under the Government of the Republic of Tajikistan. 2020. Production of Construction Materials in Tajikistan Increases Despite the Pandemic. *Agency News.* 28 April.
[73] ADB. 2019. ADB Grant to Support Tourism Development in Tajikistan. *News release.* 25 November.
[74] Government of the Republic of Tajikistan. 2018. *Tourism Development Strategy for the Period Until 2030.*
[75] ADB. 2019. Republic of Tajikistan: Tourism Development Project. Project Readiness Financing Report. Manila.

Dushanbe has a radial shape extending out of a central core area. Founded in 1925, Dushanbe consists predominantly of spontaneous individual housing developments (about 0.75 km²), medium-density Soviet micro-districts, and some administrative buildings (Figure 7). Since the early 2010s, low-rise buildings and temporary informal dwellings in the city center have been demolished to build administrative, cultural, and recreational buildings, as well as a limited number of upmarket residences. The population is increasing in the peri-urban area, where land plots can be obtained for single-family self-build. According to a government decree in 2017, Dushanbe's urban expansion is planned mainly toward the south and partly to the east and west.[76] The expansion area is limited due to the mountains in the north and existing industrial areas.

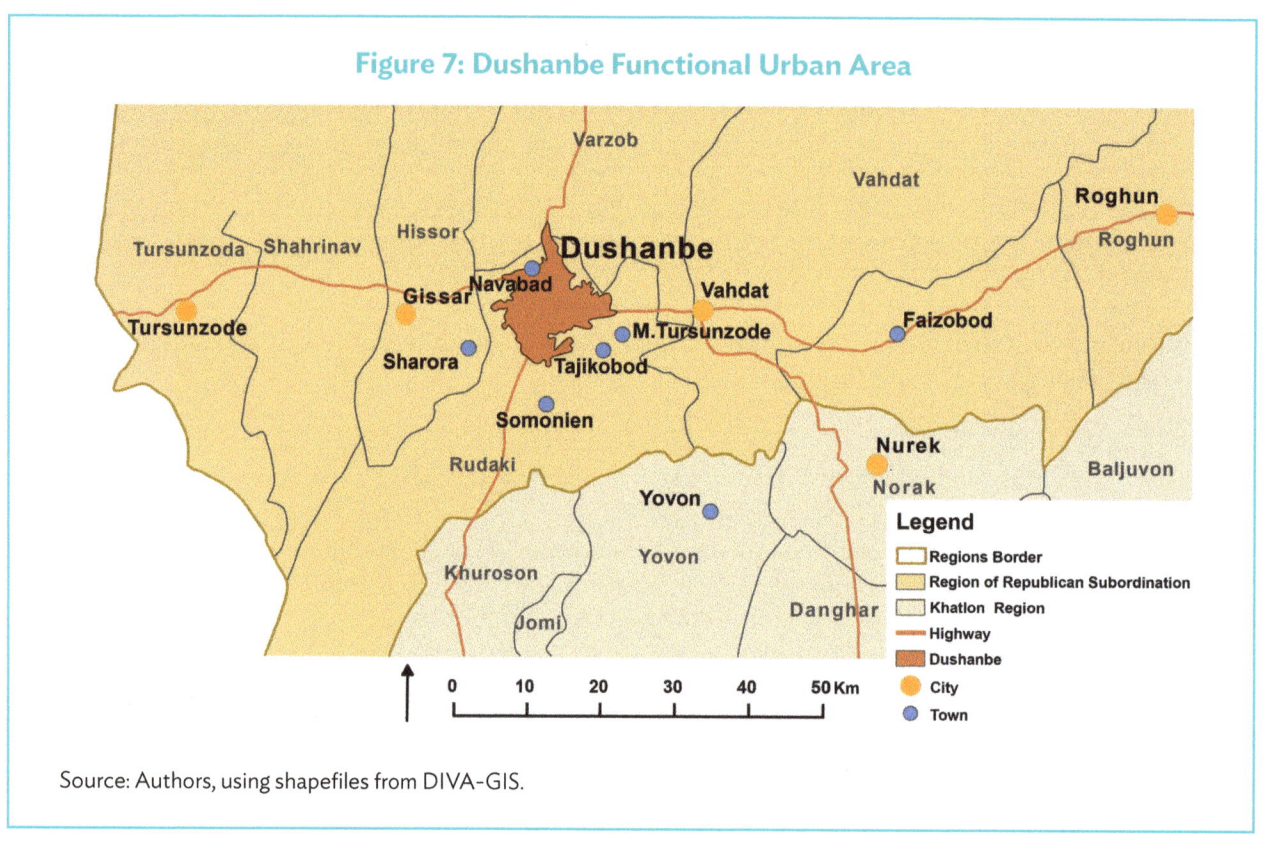

Figure 7: Dushanbe Functional Urban Area

Source: Authors, using shapefiles from DIVA-GIS.

Dushanbe has a legacy of urban sprawl, but a government resolution may change that. About 65% of residential units are single-family buildings, with the remainder multifamily. In 2010, the city area was about 120 km²,[77] and in 10 years, expanded to 203 km².[78] Map-based estimates indicate that, during this period, population density declined from 6,092 to 4,335 persons per km². However, the density decrease can also be partly explained by the 2020 annexation to the city of the adjacent Rudaki

---

[76] Decree of the Government of the Republic of Tajikistan. 2017. General Urban Plan of Dushanbe. No. 212. Dushanbe. Available in Russian.

[77] Russian State Institute for Urban Planning and Investment Development. 2009. *Correction of Master Plan of Dushanbe City, Concept of Socio-Economic and Territorial Development*.

[78] Consultations with the executive body of the state authority in Dushanbe.

district, located in the southwest. The predominance of single-family buildings has resulted in a low-density, sprawling spatial pattern. Given the limited arable land available, the introduction of Resolution 335 in 2018 intends to "protect, rationally and effectively use irrigated agricultural land, and prevent the reduction of agricultural land areas."[79] The resolution demands that all new constructions in urban central areas and the main avenues of the administrative centers of cities and districts be at least five stories. This will increase the density in urban cores, already visible in Dushanbe and Khujand, and eventually induce a compact pattern. The resolution acknowledges that urban planning documents and regulations will need to be revised to accommodate its implementation.

The predominant building typology consists of single- and two-story residential structures and self-built temporary informal dwellings. Another important part of the urban fabric is the five- and nine-story residential micro-districts built during the Soviet period. Urban renewal programs in the last decade aimed to replace informal houses with modern multistory buildings. Taller residential buildings are scattered all over the city. Light industries—garment factories, dairy plants, food factories, wineries, and beer breweries—are also found throughout the urban area. The industrial and communal area of the city accounts for about 35% of its land size. The area allocated to green space represents 19%; information on public space area and ratio is not available.

Khujand is the main agglomeration in the north of the country. The capital of the Sugd region, Khujand (with a population of 185,500) is located on the Syr Darya River in the Fergana Valley, near the borders with Uzbekistan and the Kyrgyz Republic. Khujand is the center of an agglomeration that includes nearby towns like Buston, Istiqlol, Mehrobod, Navkat, and Qayroqqum; as well as Gafurov, Jabbor Rasulov, and Spitamen (Figure 8). The population comprises about 554,000, with the surrounding districts registering average annual growth rates of over 2.0% from 2000–2021 (Table 8).[80] The cities in the Khujand area specialize in the production of construction materials and garments and metallurgy. The city has a good rail connection with Kazakhstan, the Russian Federation, and Uzbekistan. The Dushanbe–Chanak Highway, which spans the length of the country from Dushanbe in the south to the northern border with Uzbekistan, allows traveling to and from neighboring countries and Dushanbe in about 5 hours (Figure 9).[81] Air travel between the capital and the main hub in the north is limited to one flight per week and unreliable due to frequent delays or cancellations.

Khujand's spatial pattern is low density. The city area is 39.9 km² and the estimated population density is 4,649 persons per km². Like Dushanbe, Khujand mostly consists of single-family houses (including low-rise buildings, homestead-type buildings, and temporary informal dwellings). The urban pattern can be characterized by a disordered road system that negotiates its way among low-density residential areas.

---

[79] Government of the Republic of Tajikistan. Resolution Number 335. Dated June 21, 2018. On construction of at least five-story residential buildings in administrative centers of cities and districts of the Republic of Tajikistan (unofficially translated).

[80] Data is from the map-based estimates prepared for this report. See Table 4 for details.

[81] Financed and constructed by the China Road and Bridge Corporation.

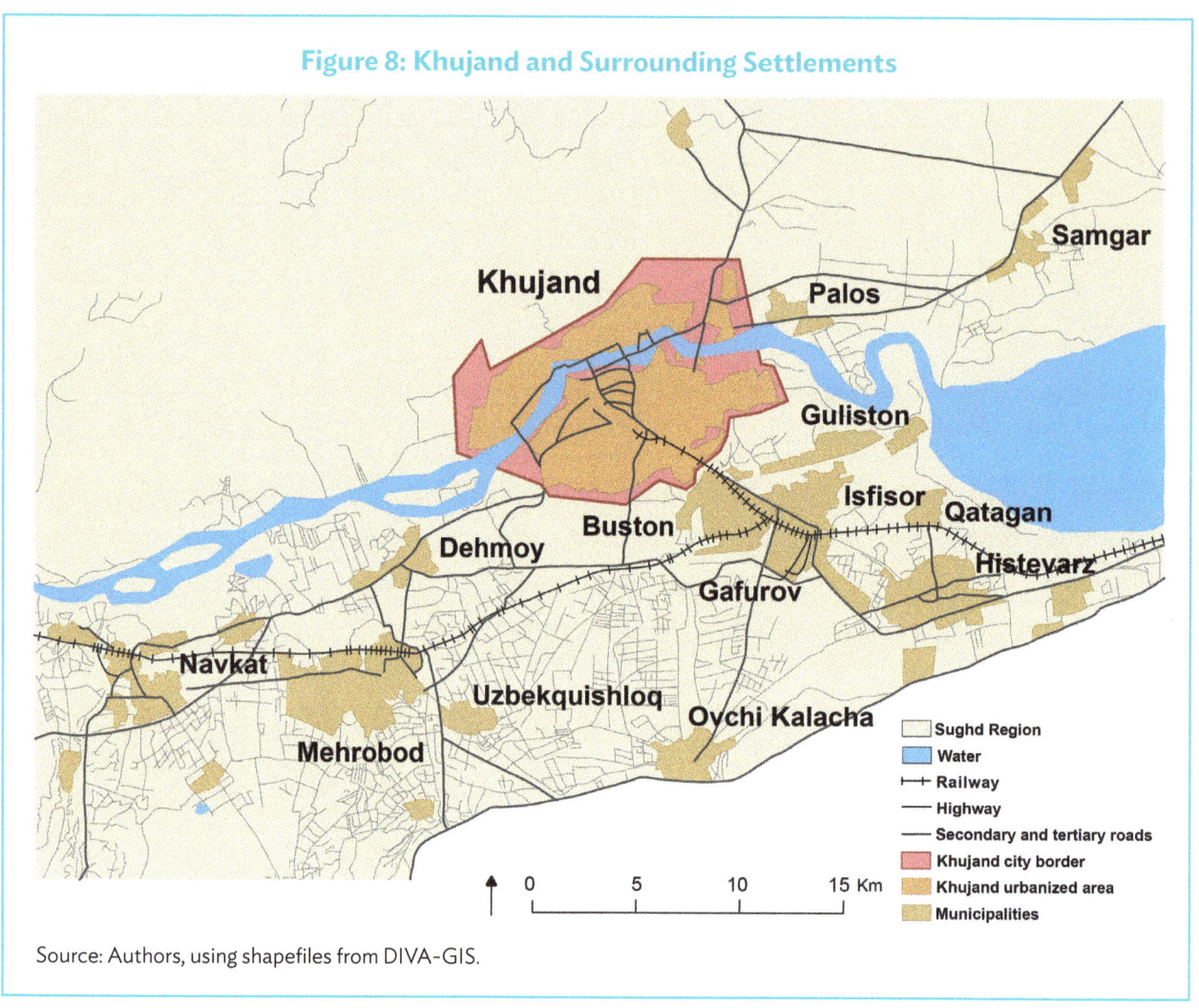

Figure 8: Khujand and Surrounding Settlements

Source: Authors, using shapefiles from DIVA-GIS.

Table 8: Population Growth Rate in Settlements Around Khujand, 2000–2021

Districts	Growth Rate 2000–2021 (%)
Spitamen	48
Jabbor Rasulov	43
Mastchoh	54

Source: Agency on Statistics under the President of the Republic of Tajikistan. 2021. *Demographic Yearbook of the Republic of Tajikistan, 30th Anniversary of State Independence, 2021* (available in hard copy only).

The core city area presents administrative and cultural buildings along the riverbank, as well as of one- to three-story buildings. Soviet micro-districts constitute a small part of the city and are mainly located on the left bank of the Syr Darya River. The city is organized around Ismoili Somoni Avenue. The airport and train station are situated outside of the city's administrative area, in Buston and Gafurov. Industrial areas are concentrated near the transport node and near the river.

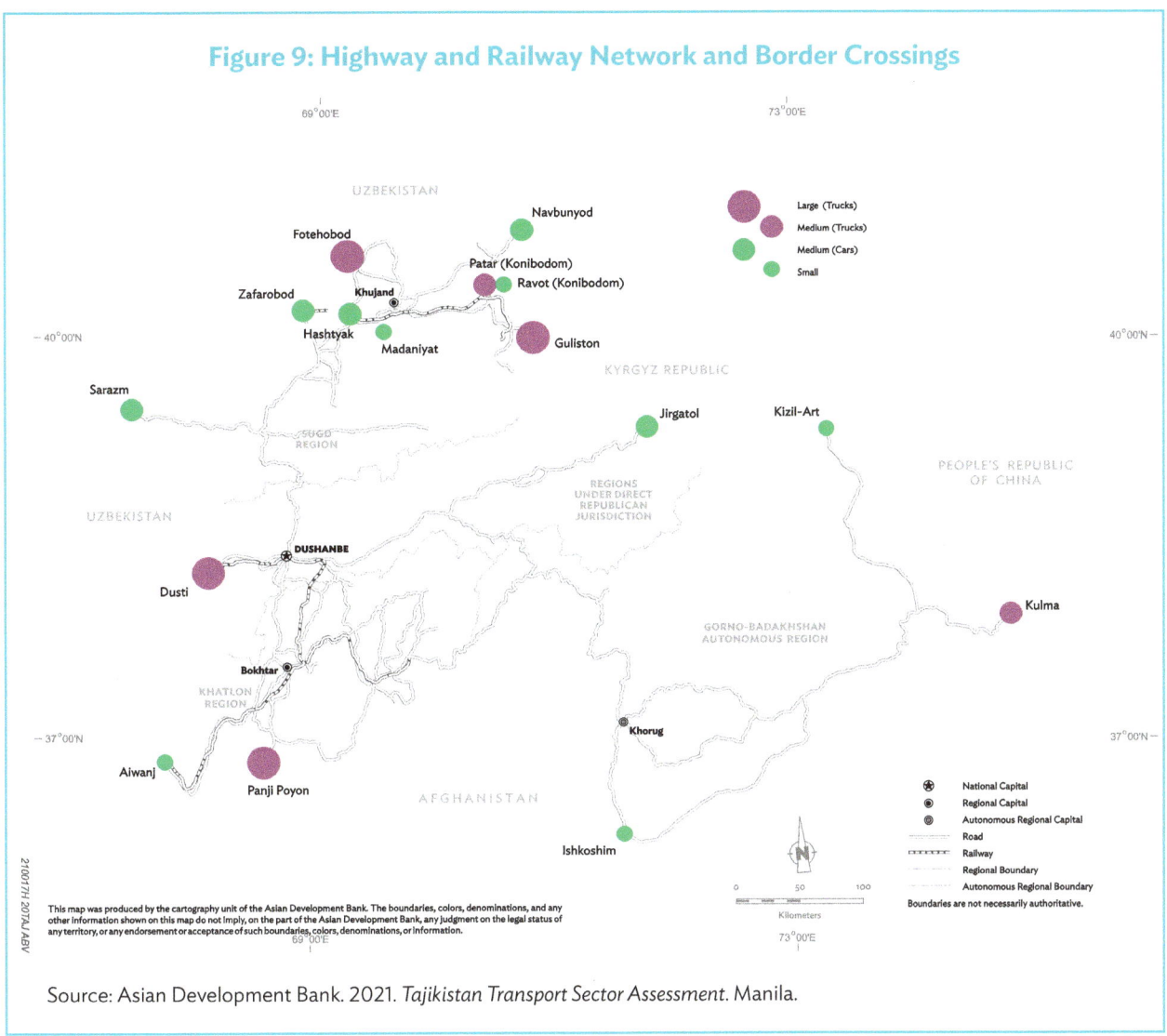

Figure 9: Highway and Railway Network and Border Crossings

Source: Asian Development Bank. 2021. *Tajikistan Transport Sector Assessment*. Manila.

Bokhtar has a relatively compact core but an expanding periphery. Located in a valley southwest of the Khatlon region, Bokhtar is divided by an irrigation canal of the nearby Vakhsh River. It has an area of 26 km², a population of 113,400, and a population density of 4,361 persons per km². From 2000 to 2021, the population grew by 46.6%. The city is surrounded by a few rural settlements and Sarband, a small city (with 17,300 inhabitants) that has an important chemical industry. Bokhtar has road and rail connections with Dushanbe (100 kilometers [km] away), Kulob (89 km away), and some Russian cities.[82] The pattern in the core area is relatively compact and organized, delimited by a ring road. The central administrative area is located at the intersection of three highways and a river. Most structures consist of Soviet micro-districts with five-story blocks, while low-density structures are prevalent in the extension outside the core. Industrial areas are situated in the city periphery near the ring road.

---

[82] During the Soviet period, there were flights between Bokhtar and Dushanbe.

Kulob has a dispersed pattern at the foot of a mountainous area. Tajikistan's fourth-biggest city is in the southwest portion of the Khatlon region. The city area is 35 km², its population is 107,700, and its population density is 3,077 persons per km². The urban population growth in the last two decades was 27.5%. Kulob is the center of a district of the same name which comprises four village communities with about 110,000 inhabitants and an area of 276 km².[83] The city has road, rail, and air communication at national and international levels. The train station is located inside the city, while the airport is about 9 km away. The urban structure is organized along Ismoili Somoni Avenue and radial roads which connect with the surrounding rural mountainous area. Kulob has predominantly low-density housing with an organic and chaotic road network. The housing pattern is more dispersed toward the mountainous fringes. Soviet micro-districts constitute a small part of the city. Industry is not widely developed and consists of small factories for food and cotton production. To attract more industries, a government program created in 2019 a special free economic zone of 309 ha next to the airport.

Tursunzoda's low-density pattern extends the built-up area to surrounding towns. It is in the Hissor Valley, in the southwest of the DRS, 55 km from Dushanbe, and not far from the border with Uzbekistan. The city area is 24.5 km², the population is 57,100, and the population density is about 2,330 persons per km². Tursunzoda is surrounded by various village communes that form the Tursunzoda district, which has about 250,000 inhabitants. The city has road and rail connection with Dushanbe, Kulob, Bokhtar, and some cities in Uzbekistan. It has a linear structure around the main urban road. Most housing areas are low-story in relatively orderly rectangular parcels. There are three micro-districts built during the Soviet period. The rail tracks limit the urban area to the south. The station is next to a large bazaar which creates a busy area in the city center. New nine- to 12-story buildings are being built in the peri-urban areas of the city. The Tajik Aluminum industrial area is in the northern part, separated from the city's built-up area, while light industrial facilities are situated inside the city. All industrial areas have railway connections.

2.5 Subsector Assessment

Transport

The urban road system has uneven quality and maintenance standards. Tajikistan's cities have well-maintained "protocol" roads, which cross the city and have a strong representative function, with a linear composition of medium- and high-rise buildings that give them a monumental image. Roads in central areas are usually in a good state. The construction and maintenance of representative roads are the responsibility of the national government. In general, the state of secondary roads tends to be uneven, whereas tertiary roads, which comprise a significant part of the urban road network, are in poorer shape. The main problem is the deterioration of asphalt surfaces with cracks and potholes. The lack of drainage in some roads contributes to rapid

---

[83] Village communities (jamoats) are the third level administrative division (after city and towns) in Tajikistan. See Figure 4 for an overview.

deterioration. Internal residential roads usually do not have proper road maintenance, such as lighting, asphalting, and cleaning of roadside ditches and trenches. While responsibility for national roads and primary urban streets falls under the Ministry of Transport, the construction and maintenance of secondary and tertiary streets falls to the municipalities. Financing comes from the district and city budget, while road planning, construction, and repair are realized by the city road management departments.

Increased motorization contributes to greater emissions and traffic congestion. In the last two decades, Tajikistan has experienced a rapid rise in motorization. At the national level, the number of automobiles more than doubled between 2000 and 2018, reaching 43 cars per 1,000 inhabitants, with a concentration in Dushanbe at 68 cars per 1,000 inhabitants in 2018 (Table 9). The importation of automobiles from the Baltic states, the PRC, the Russian Federation, and the United Arab Emirates contributed to increased motorization. Greenhouse gas (GHG) emissions from automobiles doubled in the last decade, reaching 340,000–540,000 tons of carbon dioxide equivalent per year.[84] Transport is usually approached from an automobile-centric perspective, which focuses improvement measures on road widening. Public transport and traffic management are less prominent on the agenda.

Table 9: Registered Vehicles Per 1,000 People, 2000–2018

Region	2000	2005	2010	2015	2018
Dushanbe	24	27.0	53	67	68
DRS	23	23.0	38	40	38
Sugd	28	25.0	46	56	58
Khatlon	7	11.0	27	28	28
GBAO	15	16.8	24	36	39
Total	19	21.0	38	43	43

DRS = Districts of Republican Subordination, GBAO = Gorno–Badakhshan Autonomous *Oblast* (Mountainous Badakhshan Autonomous Region).

Source: ADB. 2021. *Tajikistan Transport Sector Assessment*. Manila.

Public transport is primarily provided by small-capacity vehicles. In large cities, urban public transport is provided by state-owned enterprises that operate large-sized buses or trolleybuses, and by private companies that operate minibuses and taxis.[85] These private companies are not subsidized by municipalities, but the fares are regulated by the government. State-owned public transport companies are financed by fare proceeds and subsidies from the municipal government. The budget of the state-owned companies is not sufficient to modernize rolling stock, which generally dates to the Soviet period. In the 1950s, trolleybuses and autobuses were the dominant travel modes but today they account for just 2% of all motorized trips.[86]

---

[84] A. Gani. 2022. As Tajikistan Reindustrialises, Citizens Feel Brunt of Worsening Air Quality. *The Third Pole*. 30 March.

[85] ADB. 2021. *Tajikistan Transport Sector Assessment*. Manila.

[86] In Dushanbe and Bishkek. Y. Yang. 2019. Toward Safer, Cleaner, and More Convenient Public Transport in Central Asian Cities. *World Bank Blogs*. 31 July.

As in many other post-Soviet countries, state-owned public transport companies collapsed in the early 1990s, and demand has been met by privately operated minibuses known as *marshrutkas*. Currently, there are about 1,550 *marshrutkas* in Dushanbe. They are popular because of their frequency of service, their ability to navigate narrow and poor-quality roads, and reach of outlying low-density areas. However, they are unsafe and relatively expensive. Their proliferation contributes to air pollution and GHG emissions, as almost 90% of the fleet consists of old, secondhand vans imported from Europe (Mercedes Sprinter) and the Republic of Korea (Hyundai Starex). In 2018, the city of Dushanbe started a gradual transition to large-capacity trolleybuses and buses operated by two state-owned companies.

Public transport in secondary cities has a lower quality of service. Public bus service is usually irregular and overcrowded, and the urban-suburban connection is insufficient. Minibuses are the main means of public transport and often the only option other than taxis or private cars. An electric trolleybus system, which leverages the availability of cheap hydro energy, is planned for Bokhtar, Kulob, Vahdat, Hissor, the Rudaki district, and Tursunzoda.[87] However, up to now, these plans are still in the research and discussion phase both at local and central levels.

Efforts to improve urban public transport in Dushanbe and Khujand are ongoing. In Khujand, the trolleybus public transport service provided by the Communal State Unitary Enterprise collapsed in the early 2000s due to insufficient finances. The city provided additional concessions to *marshrutkas* to ensure the continuity of basic transport services. Recently, increasing attention has been placed back on public transport. A project financed by the European Bank for Reconstruction and Development (EBRD) and the Swiss State Secretariat for Economic Affairs, which started in 2016, has provided investment in buses, depots, equipment for maintenance, and the development of regulatory aspects. In 2019, the EBRD arranged a financing package of $8 million for the rehabilitation of the trolleybus infrastructure in Dushanbe, with seven main trolleybus routes that can transport over 11 million passengers annually. Covered are the rehabilitation of existing power substations and the installation of feeder cables as well as trolleybus power transmission wires and poles.[88] By improving the capital's obsolete trolleybus infrastructure and making it more sustainable, the project aims to revive Dushanbe's trolleybus services as a low-carbon public transport alternative in the city.

The Ministry of Transport has commenced implementation of the Comprehensive Program for the Development of Electric Transport for 2022–2026. The program, adopted on 31 October 2022 through Resolution No. 532, seeks to harness the advantages of electric transport, including higher productivity, lower emissions of GHG and harmful substances, reduced air pollution, improved urban environment, and improved road safety. It builds on the experience in developed countries where electric transport (including cars, trams, trolleybuses, metro, and trains) accounts

---

[87] Ministry of Transport of Tajikistan Republic. 2011. State Target Program for the Development of the Transport Complex in Republic of Tajikistan until 2025 (Order 165/2011). *Climate Change Laws of the World*. Grantham Research Institute on Climate Change and the Environment. London School of Economics.

[88] A. Usov. 2019. EBRD Helps Develop Dushanbe Trolleybus Network. *EBRD News*. 2 October.

for half of passenger traffic. Successful program implementation will increase to 15% the share of electric transport in the overall vehicle structure, presently significantly made up of personal cars and light commercial electric vehicles. The program foresees the production of electric vehicles in Tajikistan, including the manufacture by the Akia Avesto Avtomativ Industry LLC of 250 passenger electric transport units per year. The Ministry of Energy and Water Resources will be responsible for the development of the charging stations network. The tariff for charging, to be set by Barqi Tojik, is anticipated to be differentiated by the type of charging stations, which will significantly differ in their cost, maintenance, and charging speed. Currently, the tariff for electric transport (trolleybus) is the same as for household consumers, at $0.022 per kilowatt-hour.

Water Supply and Sanitation

A drinking water shortage has long been a problem in Tajikistan. Although the country has immense high-quality water resources, access to drinking water is still not a reality for many.[89] Water is drawn from surface water sources, and about 40% of the volume collected does not undergo the required treatment processes.[90] The deterioration of water supply and sewerage pipes and facilities contributes to water pollution as a secondary source. The sanitation system is also deteriorating, heightening the risk of water pollution and threats to public health. As a result, waterborne diseases like bacterial diarrhea, hepatitis A, and typhoid fever continue to be a major concern and account for over 3.7% of deaths.[91] In mid-1996, a multidrug-resistant typhoid fever epidemic, associated with municipal water consumption, began in southern Tajikistan. By February 1997, the epidemic had reached Dushanbe, where 8,901 cases and 95 deaths were reported from January to June 1997.[92]

While water supply and sanitation are erratic, their use intensity is high. Cities are not fully provided with centralized water and sanitation systems. An exception is Dushanbe where, apart from new development areas in the southeast, most residents have household access to water from the state unitary enterprise (SUE) *Dushanbevodokanal* (footnote 54). Public access to centralized water supply systems is 57% nationally and 91% for the urban population. Urban population increase and low-density sprawl exacerbate water supply and sanitation issues. Nonrevenue water due to leakage and commercial losses averaged 50% in Dushanbe in 2020. Aging and obsolete water supply infrastructure contribute to water losses, which amounted to 60% in urban areas in 2015.[93] Due to the limited number of wastewater treatment plants, wastewater and stormwater are not recycled. An unsustainable

---

[89] Sector Assessment (Summary): Water and Other Urban Infrastructure and Services (Urban Water Supply and Urban Sanitation). In ADB. 2022. *Report and Recommendation of the President to the Board of Directors. Proposed Grant for Additional Financing. Republic of Tajikistan: Dushanbe Water Supply and Sanitation Project.* Manila.

[90] G.D. Azimov and K.N. Daburov. 2016. *Drinking Water Supply to Population of Tajikistan. Analysis and Strategy for Future.* Eurasian Union of Scientists. #7 (28). pp. 9–11. Available in Russian.

[91] K. Hayes. 2017. Common Diseases in Tajikistan. *The Borgen Project*.12 September.

[92] J. Mermin et al. 1999. A Massive Epidemic of Multidrug-Resistant Typhoid Fever in Tajikistan Associated with Consumption of Municipal Water. *The Journal of Infectious Diseases*. 179 (6). pp. 1416–1422. June.

[93] Government of the Republic of Tajikistan. 2015. Water Reform Program of the Republic of Tajikistan for 2016–2025. Available in Russian.

water consumption pattern also harms water affordability, especially in water used for household purposes. Estimated at 0.33 cubic meters (m³) per person per day on average,[94] Tajikistan's water intensity exceeds the subregional and regional averages by over 20 times (footnote 47).

Most water pipelines are technically outdated and need repair. According to the government, 7% of the country's water infrastructure functions partially and 25% does not (footnote 90). Countrywide, water is provided by central water supply in-house connections and streetside standpipes. The central water supply service is irregular, and long periods of interrupted service are not infrequent. Several areas have only intermittent supply of 6–8 hours per day (footnote 54). A high number of users still rely on water from land-based sources like wells and rivers, which are not suitable for drinking. Water treatment and cleaning processes are poorly developed, with water processing usually stopped at the pre-chlorination stage. River water is used directly for centralized water supply (footnote 90).

The centralized sewerage system is not accessible to most people. It covers only 15% of the country's population, 53.7% in cities.[95] About 1% of the urban population relies on septic tanks, and about 45.7% use latrines and other facilities. As cities have a significant number of single-family houses, the centralized sewerage system must cover larger built-up areas. About 50% of the sewerage system in cities and peri-urban areas is not regularly functioning.[96] Poor sewerage conditions, with seepages from septic tanks and pit latrines, contribute significantly to water contamination.[97] Effluents are discharged to rivers without proper treatment. The centralized sewerage systems in the cities were built during the Soviet period, and lack of finances has impeded their maintenance and modernization. The sewerage system in Dushanbe, for example, was built in the 1970s. Rehabilitation has been taking place in the city and regional towns through the ADB-supported Dushanbe Water Supply and Sanitation Project (2018) and Additional Financing (2022), the World Bank, the EBRD, and the Swiss State Secretariat for Economic Affairs. Despite these investments, sanitation problems remain (footnote 54).

Public utility companies lack financial resources, and low tariff revenue does not cover expenses to perform maintenance works. Municipal financing is insufficient, and private investment is negligible. Tariff collection is limited,[98] and in 2016, only 58% of Tajik households reported paying for drinking water, of which 88% were urban.[99]

---

[94] ADB. 2016. *Asian Water Development Outlook 2016. Strengthening Water Security in Asia and the Pacific*. Manila.

[95] Decree of the Government of the Republic of Tajikistan. 2006. Programme for the Improvement of Clean Drinking Water Supply to the Population of the Republic of Tajikistan for the Period 2007–2020. 2 December. No. 514. Dushanbe.

[96] CAREC and UNICEF. 2021. *The Development of Sustainable Water and Sanitation Systems in Rural Areas of the CAREC Region with a Focus on China, Mongolia, Tajikistan and Uzbekistan*. Xinjiang: CAREC Institute and Beijing: UNICEF China.

[97] ADB. 2018. *Report and Recommendations of the President. Proposed Grant. Republic of Tajikistan: Dushanbe Urban Water Supply and Sanitation Project*. Manila.

[98] All tariffs in Tajikistan are set by the State Antimonopoly Agency.

[99] World Bank. 2017. *Glass Half Full: Poverty Diagnostic of Water Supply, Sanitation, and Hygiene Conditions in Tajikistan*. Washington, DC.

Water and sewerage infrastructure reconstruction needs effort and financing to be resolved (footnote 93). ADB's Dushanbe Water Supply and Sanitation Project, which supports the rehabilitation and expansion of water and sewerage network in selected districts, and assists in system management, has improved water supply for more than 100,000 people and improved sewerage for more than 350,000. The project has developed a sustainable model for climate-resilient water supply and sanitation infrastructure that can be applied across the city in the future. An Additional Financing Project, approved in August 2022, features nonrevenue water reduction through network rehabilitation as one of its key components. The EBRD, through the Green City Action Plan currently being prepared, is providing technical assistance to Dushanbe for the identification of priority projects in water supply, sanitation, and other sectors such as energy, public transport, buildings, industry, land use, and biodiversity.

Housing

Self-built houses account for about 60%–70% of the total housing stock. This can be explained by limited supply due to insufficient state housing programs and limited activity in the real estate sector, high cost of construction, and difficulties in accessing a mortgage for home buyers. Self-built houses are often constructed without projects, following general urban plans, or permits.[100] They usually have poor construction quality and are not resistant to earthquakes. Single-family houses built under a housing project approved by the architecture and urban planning authorities and with permission from the local executive body of the state authority comprise around 20%. Self-built houses represented only 13% at the end of the Soviet period. This form of delivery, which increased significantly after the civil war and reached 92% in 2000 (footnote 13), has been gradually declining and has dropped to 61.5%–62.0% in 2020 (Table 10).

Private housing construction is increasing while state construction has decreased. Housing stock commissioning increased significantly from 246,000 m^2 in 2000 to 1,463,400 m^2 in 2020 (Table 11).[101] Of this, 446,342 m^2 were in Dushanbe; 450,000 m2 in the Sugd region; 334,000 m^2 in the Khatlon region; 23,000 m^2 in GBAO; and 176,000 m^2 in the DRS.[102] The cities' housing funds and housing cooperatives decreased their contribution to housing construction from 91,500 m^2 in 2010 to 8,800 m^2 in 2020 (footnote 97).[103] The share of housing construction by enterprises and organizations, including developer companies and entrepreneurs, has been increasing, reaching over 500,000 m^2 in 2020, 62 times more than the State and Housing Cooperatives. The number of construction enterprises and organizations almost tripled in 20 years, totaling 921 in 2020 (Table 12).

---

[100] This publication refers to comprehensive, binding urban planning documents as "general plans." It is interchangeable with "master plans" frequently used in the English translation documents that were reviewed.

[101] Agency on Statistics under the President of Tajikistan. 2021. *Tajikistan: 30 Years of State Independence.* Dushanbe.

[102] Press conference by Mahmadsaid Zuvaidzoda, Head of Committee on Architecture and Construction. 4 February 2022. Dushanbe.

[103] Agency on Statistics under the President of the Republic of Tajikistan. 2021. Construction in the Republic of Tajikistan (statistical collection).

Table 10: Financing Sources of Commissioned Housing and Residential Buildings, 2020

Region	Stock Completed		
	(in 1,000 m²)	(as % of previous year)	(% share of total volume)
State	8.9	...	0.6
Foreign investment	10.3	...	0.7
Population	900.4	97.9	61.5
Limited liability company	362.0	144.9	24.7
Individual entrepreneurs	139.8	1.7	9.6
Joint stock companies	42.0	57.6	2.9
All sources	1463.4	100.5	100.0

... = no data available, m² = square meter.
Source: Authors.

Table 11: Ownership of Commissioned Residential Buildings

Year	Housing Stock Put in Operation (1,000 m²)		Population's Own-Account Share (% of total)[c]
	Enterprises and Organizations[a]	Population's Own Account[b]	
1991	1,225.2	163.5	13
1995	226.2	77.5	35
2000	245.5	226.5	92
2005	512.0	449.8	88
2010	1,029.0	826.3	80
2015	1,263.0	960.8	76
2016	338.3	847.0	72
2017	267.3	895.1	77
2018	340.5	819.1	71
2019	536.7	919.4	63
2020	562.6	900.4	62

m² = square meter.
[a] All forms, public and private, of housing enterprises, associations, and investment groups
[b] At home seekers' expense, with or without loan/s
[c] Share in total operational housing stock of units acquired at home seekers, with or without loans
Source: Agency on Statistics under the President of the Republic of Tajikistan. 2021. Construction in the Republic of Tajikistan, 2021 (statistical collection).

Table 12: Number of Construction Enterprises

	Year								
	2000	2005	2010	2015	2016	2017	2018	2019	2020
Number of construction organizations (active)	357	578	686	925	912	937	951	997	921

Source: Agency on Statistics under the President of the Republic of Tajikistan. 2021. Construction in the Republic of Tajikistan, 2021 (statistical collection).

Most existing housing stock is over 50 years old. The stock consists of single-family houses constructed under projects, self-built houses, and multifamily houses built in the Soviet period and after 1990. Around 51% of current multistory houses and 22% of single-family houses are over 50 years old, another 44% of multistory houses and 36% of single-family houses were built between 1971 and 1990, while only 5% of multifamily housing and 40% of single-family houses were built in the last 30 years.[104]

Lack of regular maintenance renders the existing multifamily houses with poor technical and sanitary conditions. In 1995, the Law on Housing Privatization enabled almost 93% of the population to acquire a housing unit. In multifamily buildings, the communal areas were divided among the private owners. Residents were responsible for the maintenance and major repairs of entrances, basements, roofs, staircases, and the surrounding area and front part of the building at their own expense.[105] Sitting tenants did not perceive they had responsibility for housing management, and in most cases, they did not have disposable income for capital repairs, which led to even more deterioration of the housing stock. The new Housing Code, which became effective in September 2022, aims to address this issue through the creation of tenants' associations for the maintenance of private residential buildings.

Developer-built multifamily buildings are required to allot social housing units from completed projects. Newly constructed multifamily houses, built mainly by private developers, usually have 9–18 floors. In exchange for using public land, these developers allocate 5%–10% of their completed units to the government for use in social housing (footnote 79). This should deliver more social housing.

Estimates of demand for housing significantly exceed supply. Although the Committee of Architecture and Construction does not have official statistics on demand, the latest projected increase in population yields a rough estimate of 70,000 additional people in need of housing every year. This is across cities of all sizes including medium and small ones.

Housing prices are not affordable for most people. The average salary is about $120–$150 per month, while the average cost per m² of a new building varies from $500 to $1,000. Prices have decreased considerably since 2016 (by about 41.6% in

---

[104] UNECE. 2017. *Tajikistan. Environmental Performance Reviews. Third Review.* Geneva.
[105] Consumers International. Consumers Union of Tajikistan.

aggregate), mainly due to shrinking remittances—the population used remittances for household needs and the excess funds were invested into new developments thus increasing demand. However, as they are mostly imported, the prices of construction materials have remained high, putting housing beyond the means of most people. Prices in the housing rental market are also incompatible with the average salary. They range from $130 to $400 per month in Dushanbe, Khujand, and Tursunzoda and start from $85 per month in Bokhtar and Kulob.

The mortgage market in Tajikistan is underdeveloped. An interest rate of around 22% per annum and short lending period in the mortgage market makes housing loans unaffordable for most citizens (Table 13). The high interest rate may be explained by high risks in debt return, an undeveloped legal framework, and financial sector management challenges (footnote 26). Microfinancing, a widely practiced and viable option in many developing countries, is also underdeveloped in Tajikistan.

Table 13: Mortgage Terms in Select Banks in Tajikistan
(as of mid-2022)

	Spitamenbank	Eskhata	Humo
Amount	$1,000–$150,000	TJS10,000–TJS350,000	TJS40,000–TJS250,000
Tenure	3 to 120 months	Up to 120 months	Up to 60 months
Down Payment	30%	30%	30%
Collateral	No	125% of real estate	Real estate
Interest rate	In $: 15%[a]	In TJS: 26%	In TJS: 30% In $: 18%

TJS = Tajikistan somoni.

[a] Spitamenbank collaborates with several developers and offers a 12% interest rate on loans arranged by these developers.

Source: Authors' calculations.

Social housing programs have limited impact. The new Housing Code has two chapters on social housing. Despite a detailed discussion, including on the acquisition procedure, state programs have not yet been fleshed out to improve the momentum of social housing provision. In the past 10 years, the program, Construction of Affordable Housing, delivered only seven multifamily apartment buildings in Dushanbe for about 850 persons.

Solid Waste Management

Solid waste management in Tajikistan is outdated and waste generated is expected to triple by 2050. Tajikistan's cities produce more than 5,500 tons per day and 2 million tons per year of solid waste. This amount is expected to almost triple by 2050 to 5.6 million tons per year (footnote 47). Solid waste is not sorted but dumped in over 70 landfills and/or open disposal sites.[106] The construction of two solid waste treatment plants, one in Khujand and another in Dushanbe, is under consideration. These government-proposed projects are expecting funding from foreign investors. Recycling is largely underdeveloped (footnote 99), and the public is not widely aware about its importance, but environmental protection departments and environmental activists are working to increase awareness. There is no national policy on recycling, only a general law about waste collection procedures. Some small private companies are engaged in recycling but no documentation is available on their operations and the amount of waste they are able to recycle. Meanwhile, there is also an unknown number of recycling points handling mercury-containing lamps in various locations.

While there is no hard data, the negative impact of poor waste disposal on public health and the environment is apparent and irrefutable. Solid waste collection services reach 80% of the urban population. In Dushanbe, the waste collection rate is 95% but in Khujand it drops to 32%.[107] The four municipal waste collection companies operating at the district level in Dushanbe, and SUE *Khizmatrasonii Naqliyoti Sanitari* operating in Khujand lack financial resources and have outdated equipment. Tariffs for solid waste are set by the municipal government and approved by the Antimonopoly Service under the national government. Tariffs are in general very low and do not meet operational costs. For residents, tariffs are set per capita per month, and for legal entities per m³ (Table 14). Disposal of hazardous materials such as batteries and chemicals is not properly organized, increasing the risk of soil contamination. The number of collection points is insufficient, resulting in long-lying waste in residential yards, streets, and open fields. New multifamily houses sometimes are also lacking waste collection sites in their courtyards. All these contribute to the rise of spontaneous rubbish sites.

Table 14: Waste Disposal Tariffs in Dushanbe Districts

	Unit	Ismoili Somoni	Shohmansur	Sino	Firdavsi
Buildings with garbage chute	pc	2.40	2.40	2.60	2.50
Buildings without garbage chute	pc	2.00	2.00	2.20	2.10
Temporary informal dwellings	pc	2.70	2.70	3.00	2.80
Residential houses	pc	2.90	2.90	3.10	3.00
Budgetary organizations	m³	23.00	23.00	27.00	27.00
Commercial enterprises	m³	27.00	27.00	39.00	39.00

m³ = cubic meter, pc = per capita.

Source: Executive Body of State Authority in Dushanbe (unofficial translation of Russian agency name).

---

[106] N. Karimov. 2021. Bury and Forget: How People "Struggle" with Growth of Landfills in Tajikistan. *Central Asian Bureau for Analytical Reporting.* 1 April.

[107] S. Kaza et al. 2018. What a Waste 2.0. A Global Snapshot of Solid Waste Management to 2050. *Urban Development Series.* World Bank. Washington, DC.

Energy

The electricity supply is unreliable and inefficient. Accessibility problems are caused by unstable sources and outdated infrastructure. Tajikistan is over 90% dependent on hydroelectric power. Due to the lack of water in rivers in winter, around 70% of the population experience electricity shortages, with supply available only 6–7 hours per day (footnote 47). Electricity supply problems have become more frequent in the last decade, and the aging infrastructure, poor maintenance, and overloaded transmission and distribution systems have led to electricity losses of about 18%–22%.

Electricity is subsidized by the government, and tariffs are not sufficient to support maintenance and reconstruction works. Electricity tariffs are low and do not cover operational and capital expenditures. Imported gas has higher tariffs than electricity, increasing the electricity demand. The current tariff policy does not adequately address the need to expand the revenue base and recover expenditures. The state company Barqi Tojik has a monopoly electricity supply, creating difficulties for private investment.

While energy consumption has declined, the country's energy efficiency approach continues to lack scope. In 2000, Tajikistan's energy usage was higher than the North and Central Asia average. The country has since reduced consumption, which is now lower than the regional average (footnote 47). Since 2010, power consumption per capita has declined from 1,843 to 1,616 kilowatt-hours.[108] One measure that significantly helped was the installation of smart metering systems in households, which account for about 30% of the total electricity consumption.[109] However, there is still much scope to control commercial energy losses by offering energy efficiency initiatives to the industry and agriculture sectors. Electricity consumption in these sectors comprises about 70% of the total. Inefficient and aging electricity-intensive technologies, including the old irrigation systems widely used in agriculture, will have to be replaced to drastically cut the country's energy use.

District Heating

The district heating system is inadequate and unreliable. The centralized heating system is an organized public service, but only 9% of the population, predominantly in cities, is connected to the system.[110] Usually, the heating season in Tajikistan starts on 15 October and ends on 15 March. Constructed more than 30 years ago, this heating system has endured poor maintenance, and is currently deteriorated. Unused heating infrastructure was dismantled by flat owners and large investments are required to recover the service. In 2021, the EBRD provided a financial package of $10 million (a $5 million loan and $5 million grant) to the District Heating Company of Dushanbe to restore, upgrade, and extend the existing district heating network and overhaul pumping stations.[111]

---

[108] countryeconomy.com. Tajikistan – Electricity Consumption (accessed 22 June 2022).
[109] This measure was realized with the support of the World Bank during 2005–2012.
[110] United Nations Economic and Social Commission for Asia and the Pacific. 2015. *Case Study: Tajikistan. Energy Production and Consumption Sector*. Bangkok.
[111] A. Usov. 2021. EBRD Supports District Heating Upgrade in Dushanbe. *EBRD News*. 14 April.

The lack of a centralized heating service forces people to search for other energy resources. Apart from centralized heating, urban multifamily houses use electricity for heating, while single-family houses use electricity, coal, and wood. Such intensive use of electricity for heating, which reaches almost 50% of households in urban areas, creates additional burden on the already weak electricity supply.[112] The urban population, including those living in multifamily and administrative buildings, also rely on individual solutions for heating. Heaters and electric oil radiators usually have high fuel consumption and contribute negatively to air quality.

Thermal efficiency is low in about 90% of houses. This was established by a UN case study on the country's energy consumption (footnote 110). Existing houses have poor thermal insulation, high air permeability, and insufficient maintenance. Old houses and self-built houses have high energy losses as well as newly built single-family and multifamily houses. There are cases in which construction permits are issued without proper control of existing energy efficiency norms and standards.

The existing tariff system is not sufficient to ensure proper maintenance and repair work. The tariff for heating is based on the square meterage of a dwelling and not on consumption. Even if the tariffs are low and insufficient for public companies, they may represent a significant percentage of household income. Companies receive subsidies from national and city budgets to cover more than 50% of their budget needs. Subsidies are used to cover operational costs of maintenance and priority repairs.

2.6 Urban Environment

Air and water pollution are the main urban environmental concerns. In 2021, Tajikistan ranked as the fourth most polluted country in the world (footnote 84). Air quality in cities is generally poor, although Dushanbe has a moderate pollution level, with a yearly particulate matter 2.5 average reading of 20 micrograms per m^3. GHG emissions from automobiles have doubled in the last decade, reaching 340,000–540,000 tons of carbon dioxide. Cities continue to have automobile-oriented planning, which implies more road construction projects, while public transport receives a secondary role. Air quality is deteriorating due to the intensive use of coal and wood for heating in the cities. Intensive industrialization based mostly on outdated equipment is also heavily polluting the air. Dushanbe, for example, has industries with high dust emissions, like cement and coal plants. Pollution is exacerbated by the low proportion of green public space.

Urban environmental livability requires public, green, and pedestrian space development. Segregated zoning is still used as a main planning approach in Tajikistan cities. This prevents cities from having mixed-use areas. Wide streets intensify the separation between buildings and diminish the cohesion of the urban fabric. A pedestrian-friendly approach to infrastructure (for example, crossings with priority, accessibility of amenities, and pedestrian walking corridors) is still to be

---

[112] World Bank. 2015. *Reliable and Affordable Heating is Essential to Everyday Life in Tajikistan.* Feature Story. 23 July.

developed. Urban rivers and water bodies usually are not integrated into city planning for water management nor recreational space purposes, and riverbank areas lack attractive public space and amenities. There is also a lack of information on green space availability in the cities, except in Dushanbe, where this may be gleaned from documented land use patterns (Table 15).

Table 15: Land Use in Dushanbe

Land	Area (ha)
Irrigated land	2,091.75
Orchards	145.21
Silk gardens	12.28
Citrus orchards	2.10
Pastures	25.79
Settlements	6,390.85
Private farms/gardens	65.79
Swamp	3.70
Bush thickets	1,372.00
Reservoirs	1,436.66
Underground passages	310.20
Construction	7,227.51
Land not used for agriculture	1,235.03

ha = hectare.

Sources: *Vecherka*. 2020. Geography of Dushanbe in Numbers. 27 July; and Executive Body of State Authority of Dushanbe (unofficial translation of Russian agency name).

Anthropogenic disasters in industry and agriculture are widespread in Tajikistan. At least 10% of the population lives on degraded lands (footnote 25). Chemical plants and industrial waste disposal sites in the Sugd region are in a natural hazard zone. The intensive use of the valleys for agriculture, because of the scarcity of arable lands, contributes to erosion and soil salinization.

2.7 Urban Governance and Management Profile

Institutions Guiding Urban Development

Urbanization is managed at the central government level. Land management and the registration of land use rights are with the State Committee for Land Management and Geodesy of the Republic of Tajikistan. The state committee has authorized SUE

"Registration of Immovable Property" to prepare documents for the registration of land use rights. This SUE also takes charge of surveying land plots and preparing and issuing Land Use Right Certificates. The SUE has 69 offices located in all districts and cities. While it assists in documentation requirements, *hukumats* decide on the allocation of land use rights. The design and research institute FAZO, also under the State Committee for Land Management, is the leading organization for geographic information systems and delimitation of maps.

The activities of several institutions responsible for land administration are not well coordinated. Data integration is insufficient, sharing processes are underdeveloped, and an effective cadastre and registration system has not yet been implemented due to the lack of financial, technical, and human resource capacities (footnote 25).

Land Administration and Land Markets

Land is the property of the state, and the right to use it can be transferred. The 1994 Constitution and several laws, presidential decrees, and administrative regulations govern land rights in Tajikistan (footnote 25). The Land Code establishes that "land is the exclusive property of the state, and the state guarantees its effective use for the benefit of the people." [113] It was first adopted in 1996 and amended seven times, with the last amendment in 2016. The 1996 Land Code reaffirmed state ownership of land and made provisions to secure the rational use and protection of land. The present code stipulates allowing individuals to collateralize and sell their land use rights under land tenure types created by previous laws (footnote 25). The code defines land use rights as the acquired right of indefinite, temporary, or lifelong hereditary use or based on a lease agreement of a plot of land (footnote 112).

Several Land Code dispositions are, on paper, favorable for the development of a land market. For example, Article 13 of the Land Code cites the necessity of organizing a land use rights market to support its effective operation and prevent monopolistic activities, acknowledges the element of profitability in land use, and indicates that information on land plots must be available. These legal dispositions coexist with what can be considered planned economy practices. For example, the government has the power to determine land use change from agricultural to non-agricultural when it deems necessary, so in practice, *hukumats* can specify the use of land at their discretion. The code also expands the justification for the compulsory acquisition of land to include the establishment and/or expansion of a city or settlement area.

The transfer of land rights is carried out by executive bodies of the state authority, but their coordination and capacity are suboptimal. According to the Land Code, land plot boundaries are to be delimited by *hukumats*.[114] The Law on Land Valuation has established the individual cadastral land assessment as a basis for determining the price of a specific parcel of land, considering, among various factors, changes in

---

[113] Government of Tajikistan. 2016. *Kodeksi Zamini Juhurii Tojikiston* (Land Code of the Republic of Tajikistan, unofficially translated).
[114] Official Gazette 05.01.08, No. 357.

supply and "operating market prices."[115] The local executive bodies of state authority of districts and cities, with the agreement of local land development authorities, can issue Land Use Right Certificates for indefinite, temporary, and lifetime hereditary use. Land plots can be given to foreign citizens and foreign legal entities for temporary use for up to 50 years. Land in populated areas (cities, towns, and rural settlements) is to be transferred in plots of up to 10 hectares.

The current property registration process in Tajikistan is complex. In the 2020 Doing Business survey of 190 economies, Tajikistan ranked 137th in terms of property registration.[116] It performed below neighboring Central Asia countries, and its rank declined from 77th in 2010. Registration requires 26 procedures compared with 16 on average in Central Asia. Constraints include the duplication of registration data and the fact that the land-parcel-based system has yet to be completed (footnote 26). Progress since then has been insufficient.

Real estate is constrained by high costs and an immature mortgage market. The high price of housing is exacerbated by the exorbitant cost of construction materials, about 80% of which are imported.[117] It is nearly impossible for most people to obtain a mortgage loan, and the complex procedure makes it even more expensive. This means that home buyers must pay for housing entirely up front, the extreme difficulty of which has resulted in the proliferation of self-constructed units in peri-urban land.

Urban Planning and Management

Urban planning is centralized and carried out by state authorities. The state, through the State Committee for Land Management and Geodesy, is the only owner of land in the country. It executes every step in the urban planning process, working through well-delineated authorities and a hierarchical authority system (Figure 10). The Committee on Architecture and Construction (CAC), under the president, is the dedicated state agency for planning cities, towns, and other populated areas, as well as issuing licenses for construction activities. *Shahrofar*, a design institute under the CAC, prepares the urban planning documentation requirements, including general plans, detailed plans, and district planning schemes. Founded in 1930, it has six production departments and about 115 staff with professionally qualified architects and urban planners. From 2003 to 2017, it was engaged in the adjustment and development of general plans for 59 settlements.

The incomplete transition to a market-based land development system has created an ad hoc approach to urban planning and management. After the collapse of the Soviet Union and the emergence of new political and economic systems, urban planning activities began to be poorly financed by the state. The general plans of cities and towns became outdated and ceased to correspond to real conditions.

---

[115] Commonwealth of Independent States (CIS) Legislation. Law of the Republic of Tajikistan about Land Assessment.

[116] World Bank Group. 2020. *Economy Profile. Tajikistan. Doing Business 2020.*

[117] Transmission. RadioFreeEurope.RadioLiberty 2011. *The Sky High Price of Real Estate in Dushanbe.* 29 September.

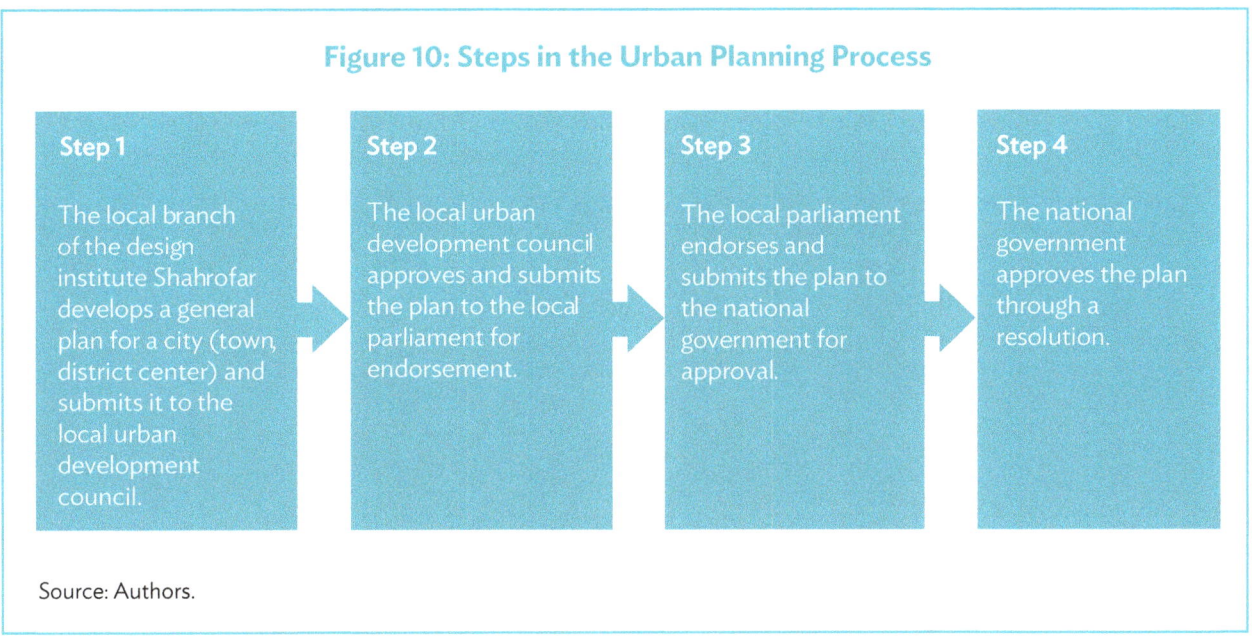

Figure 10: Steps in the Urban Planning Process

Step 1
The local branch of the design institute Shahrofar develops a general plan for a city (town, district center) and submits it to the local urban development council.

Step 2
The local urban development council approves and submits the plan to the local parliament for endorsement.

Step 3
The local parliament endorses and submits the plan to the national government for approval.

Step 4
The national government approves the plan through a resolution.

Source: Authors.

The current general plans of cities were mostly developed and approved in 1973–1985. New plans for cities started to be developed only in 2005. Current methods present several issues. Self-construction of individual residential buildings is often carried out without coordinating the building plan and design with the architectural service of the local authorities. The Strategy for the Development of the Construction Industry identifies non-compliance with government plans as a key problem caused by self-constructed residences (footnote 13). Urban land, meant to be regulated by the general plan, is often not used according to its intended function or real value. Land plots for construction purposes are lacking. Plot boundaries are often infringed, and land is occupied. There is poor transparency in the procedures for setting the cost of the transfer of land rights.[118]

2.8 Urban Finance Profile

Public Finance Management

The public finance management system in Tajikistan is centralized, with no municipal autonomy. The Constitution is the basis of the procedures for the establishment and operation of higher public authorities and their relationships and competence focuses, hence, also the basis for the structure and structural relationship among entities involved in public finance management (PFM)

---

[118] UNECE. 2014. Resolution of the Dushanbe Workshop "Strengthening National Capacities for Sustainable Housing, Energy Efficiency and Urban Planning". 28–29 October. Dushanbe.

(Table 16). The primary responsibility for PFM lies with the Ministry of Finance (MOF).[119] As part of strategic planning, the ministry works with the Ministry of Economic Development and Trade and the National Bank of Tajikistan. The Budget Commission sets budget priorities, approves the draft budget, and submits it to the Parliament for consideration. The government finalizes and adopts the Draft Law on the State Budget and submits it to the Parliament for further review.[120] The deadline for submitting the draft budget to Parliament each year is 1 November. The Parliament has until 31 December to review and approve the budget. In practice, the budget is approved in time for the start of the new fiscal year, 1 January.

Appendix 1 lists the main legal documents of Tajikistan on PFM.

Table 16: Responsibilities in Public Finance Management
(Other Agencies)

PFM Function	Responsible Agency
Budget planning and monitoring	Executive Office of the President
Financial control	Agency for State Financial Control and Combating Corruption
Macroeconomic forecasting, capital expenditure planning	Ministry of Economic Development and Trade
Public investment coordination and monitoring, public assets management	State Committee on Investment and Management of State Property
PFM statistics	State Statistics Committee
Public procurement	State Agency for Public Procurement of Goods, Works, and Services
Revenue administration	Tax Committee
Customs duties collection, taxes on international trade	Customs Service
External audit	Chamber of Accounts, Agency on Combating Corruption and Financial Control

PFM = public finance management.

Note: This schedule of responsibility identifies the functions and agencies supporting public finance management in Tajikistan, primary responsibility for which is with the Ministry of Finance.

Source: World Bank, SWISSAID, and United Kingdom Department of international Development. 2017. Government of Tajikistan Public Expenditure and Financial Accountability Assessment. *Country Financial Accountability Assessment.* 13 June.

---

[119] The organizational structure of the MOF is a mix of functional and divisional principles of management. It includes the minister, first deputy, and two deputy ministers. Each deputy minister leads several specific departments and reports to the minister. There are 33 units, and they directly report to the minister/deputy ministers.

[120] Tajikistan's Parliament – the Majlisi Oli – consists of two chambers, the Majlisi Milli and the Majlisi Namoyandagon. The Majlisi Milli (Upper House) is based on indirect elections by regional councils (75% of seats) and presidential appointments (25% of seats). The Majlisi Namoyandagon (Lower House) is directly elected by popular vote. Only the Lower House is directly involved in the scrutiny of the budget. The current Parliament was elected on 1 March 2020 for a 5-year tenure. Resolutions of the Lower House are passed by a majority vote of the total number of deputies, if no other procedure is provided by the Constitution. The execution of resolutions adopted by the Lower House is obligatory in Tajikistan.

Intergovernmental Transfer Mechanism

The Ministry of Finance engages directly with major subnational governments in budgeting. Article 5 of the Law on Public Finances divides the budgeting process into two levels. The first level focuses on the State Budget and budgets for the state trust funds, and the second level on the local budgets. The local budgets are for the three *oblasts*, Dushanbe and 13 other cities, and the DRS. The role of line ministries in the formulation of the budget for the different sectors of the economy has been relatively limited. Local budgets are developed by local *hukumats* and adopted by the local representative bodies of the state entities as normative legal acts.[121] Financial departments of line ministries execute their own and subordinate institutions' budgets. A significant part of services, especially social services, are provided locally and financed from local budgets. Line ministries have general information about their line institutions at the local level but do not yet fully use the financial data from these institutions for analytical or assessment purposes.

The MOF and its field treasury offices exercise control over revenues, expenditures, and State Budget performance. According to the Law on Treasury, local treasury branches directly report to the Central Treasury Office or the MOF.[122] The law also defines the roles and duties of the Central Treasury and its local branches, relationships with the banking system, management of the Treasury Single Account, and responsibility in budget organization, accounting, and reporting procedures. The working procedures of the central and local treasuries on financing, receipt of documents, expenditure and cost estimates, and types of reports on central and local budget performance are defined based on instructions approved by the MOF. The use of conservative budget estimates is a main principle in the context of the limited resources and economic vulnerability of the country. All budget entities keep their accounts in the Treasury Single Account, however, there is no single centralized database on public servants, and no single automated payroll system for public servants. Payroll accounting is decentralized, which weakens the function of central financial control and creates the conditions for manipulation of salary spending at the local level.

All public sector organizations financed from the State Budget are required to establish an internal control system. This is provided in the Internal Financial Control Law. The system includes a control environment, risk management, information and communication, and monitoring. The MOF oversees the development of financial management and internal control policy and the coordination and supervision of internal control activities in budget organizations. Public sector organizations submit their annual financial management and internal control reports to the MOF before 1 April, yearly. The MOF presents a consolidated annual financial management and internal control report to the government by 1 May.

---

[121] Article 6 of the Law on Public Finances of the Republic of Tajikistan.

[122] The powers and responsibilities of public authorities in public finance management are determined by various legal acts, including the Constitutional Law on the Government of the Republic of Tajikistan (2001), the provisions of ministries and departments that are part of the structure of public administration, the Constitutional Law on local government bodies (2004), and the Law on Self-Governance Bodies of Towns and Townships (as amended in 2009).

Enabling Environment for Own-Source Revenues

Subnational own-source revenues are limited in Tajikistan. The property tax[123] is the only source assigned to tier 2 and tier 3 subnational governments (SNGs) in the Tax Code of Tajikistan.[124] However, property tax, which is less than 10% of the total revenues, is not a significant revenue source for local governments. According to the MOF, the revenue collection rate at the local level is, on average, about 105% of what was planned. Tax is collected monthly, although MOF publishes the State Budget, including execution reports for the national and local budgets, every quarter.

Real estate in Tajikistan is taxed based on size, use, and location, not on market value. Real estate tax in the country follows a differentiated fee schedule based on area, use, and location (Table 17). It is higher in developed urban areas than in less developed ones and the rural areas. For example, in 2022, the tax for a residential flat of 100 m² in Dushanbe was 15% higher than Khujand, Bokhtar, and Kulob.[125] Regional coefficients set by the Tax Code regulate the level of real estate taxes (Table 18).

Table 17: Tax Rates by Type, Size, and Location of Real Estate

Real Estate Object	Size (m²)	Tax Rate (per m², % of set indicator)ª	Location	Note
Real estate objects used as residential buildings (premises), as well as their auxiliary buildings	< 90	3	Real estate objects located in the cities of Dushanbe, Khujand, Kulob, and Bokhtar have tax rates twice as high.	Real estate objects located in tourism and recreation development zones and used for business purposes have tax rates twice as high.
	90 to 200	4		
	> 200	6		
Real estate objects used for trading activities, establishment of public catering establishments, other types of services and performance of works	< 250	12		
	250 to 500	15		
	> 500	18		
Real estate objects used for other activities (non-commercial)	< 200	9		
	200 to 500	12		
	> 500	15		

> = greater than, < = less than, m² = square meter.
ª Indicator for calculation is set by the Government of Tajikistan (currently TJS64).
Source: Tax Code of the Republic of Tajikistan.

---

[123] Article 343 of the Tax Code of the Republic of Tajikistan defines property as real estate, land plots, and means of transportation, which are taxed on a yearly basis.
[124] Article 24 of the Tax Code of the Republic of Tajikistan.
[125] Calculations made by this report place the tax amount in Dushanbe at ((100 m² x TJS2.56) x 1 x 2) = TJS512, while in Khujand, Bokhtar, and it would be: ((100 m² x TJS2.56) x 0.8 x 2) = TJS409.60.

Table 18: Regional Coefficients Regulating Real Estate Tax Amounts

Group	Name of Cities, Districts, and Regions	Regional Coefficients
1	The territory of the city of Dushanbe	1.0
2	The territory of the cities of Bokhtar, Khujand, and Kulob	0.8
3	Administrative territory of the cities of Buston, Guliston, Hissor, Isfara, Istaravshan, Istiqlol, Khorug, Konibodom, Kushoniyon, Levakant, Norakand, Panjakent, Rogun, Tursunzoda, and Vahdat	0.6
4	Territory of other villages and administrative centers of districts not specified in groups 1, 2, or 3	0.4
5	The territory of the villages belonging to the districts (cities) of Bobojon Gafurov, Buston, Dangara, Dusti, Farkhor, Guliston, Hissor, Isfara, Istaravshan, Jabbor Rasulov, Jaloliddin Balkhi, Jayhun, Khuroson, Konibodom, Kubodyon, Kulob, Levakant, Mir Sayyid Ali Hamadoni, Muminabad, Norak, Nosiri Hisrav, Panj, Panjakent, Rudaki, Shahritus, Shakhrinav, Spitamen, Tursunzoda, Vahdat, Vakhsh, Vose, and Yavan	0.3
6	Territory of villages belonging to other areas and not listed in groups 5 or 7	0.2
7	The territory of the villages belonging to the city of Rogun, the districts of Ayni, Darvaz, Devashtich, Ishkashim, Kuhistoni Mastchokh, Murghab, Nurobod, Rasht, Roshtkala, Rushan, Shakhristan, Shugnan, and Vanch	0.1

Source: Tax Code of the Republic of Tajikistan.

The property tax on vehicles is part of the revenue of tier 2 SNGs (cities and districts). Taxpayers are owners or users of cars, motorcycles, scooters, buses, and other water and air vehicles, the list of which is determined by the government. Tax rates are set based on engine power, jet engine pressure, name, seats, carrying capacity, and other indicators. According to the Ministry of Transport, the country had 436,444 units of automobile transport, including 14,352 cargo vehicles, 9,743 passenger buses and vans, and 13,116 taxis, as of July 2017.[126]

Land tax is a revenue source for local budgets. It is based on the quality, cadastral zone, purpose of use, and environmental features of land plots. Taxpayers are land users who receive the plots for perpetual and temporary inherited lifetime use and land users who use the plots, except for producers of agricultural goods.[127] The tax is levied on land area. However, there are land tax exemptions, including on historical or cultural sites, national parks, and land used by the state.

---

[126] Ministry of Transport of the Republic of Tajikistan (available in Russian).
[127] Agriculture producers fall under a special simplified tax regime.

Tax rate per ha is set by the Government of Tajikistan every 5 years. The State Committee for Land Management and Geodesy calculates and propose the rate per ha by region and city or district considering the cadastral zone and type of land, including whether the land is suitable for settlements, forests, and agriculture (Table 19). The proposals are then submitted to the national government for approval.

Table 19: Land Tax Rates

Land type and features	Size (ha)	Tax Rate (per ha)
Land plots for houses and auxiliary buildings	< 0.12 ha irrigated and 0.15 non-irrigated land	According to rates
	0.12 to 0.2 ha irrigated and 0.15 to 0.25 non-irrigated	2 times the rates
	> 0.2 ha irrigated and 0.25 non-irrigated	3 times the rates
Land for commercial activities, excluding agricultural producers	< 0.12 ha irrigated and 0.15 non-irrigated land	5 times the rates
	0.12 to 0.2 ha irrigated and 0.15 to 0.25 non-irrigated	10 times the rates
	> 0.2 ha irrigated and 0.25 non-irrigated	15 times the rates
Land used by legal entities	< 0.12 ha irrigated and 0.15 non-irrigated land	25 times the rates
	0.12 to 0.2 ha irrigated and 0.15 to 0.25 non-irrigated	50 times the rates
	> 0.2 ha irrigated and 0.25 non-irrigated	75 times the rates

> = greater than, > = less than, ha = hectare.
Source: Tax Code of the Republic of Tajikistan.

For all other types of tax revenues, the government can adjust its annual tax-sharing arrangements. Local authorities have the right to use, at their discretion, the revenues received in excess of the approved (planned or anticipated) amounts by the MOF. But the excess amounts are often insignificant. In practice, they help to address only short-term objectives and restrict SNGs from developing their strategic plans for revenues and expenditures.

In addition to the local tax, the revenues of local budgets also include transfers, state duties, and non-tax revenues. Local tax and other mandatory payments to the local budget are defined by Article 12 of the Law on Public Finances. Revenues from regulated state taxes are defined and transferred to local governments in accordance with the Law on State Budget for the following fiscal year. Non-tax revenues from the state budget consist of grants, subventions, subsidies, as well as mutual financial settlements; payments from the lease of local property; revenues from paid services rendered by local executive bodies of state authority; budgetary institutions funded from the local budget; revenues from other legitimate sources including fines, penalties, and interests for violation of contractual obligations; compensation for damage caused to local budgets as a result of violation of financial discipline; revenues from extrabudgetary sources such as grants and other gratuitous receipts from individuals, legal entities and international organizations; and revenues from regulated state taxes and other payments (Table 20).

Table 20: Local Revenues, Quarter 1, 2022
(TJS million)

Revenues[a]	Planned	Collected	%
TAX REVENUES	1,727.60	1,818.00	105.20
(i) Income tax	761.10	785.90	102.50
Personal income tax	403.40	400.40	99.30
Income tax from legal entities	363.70	385.5	106.00
(ii) Property tax	179.30	207.50	115.70
(iii) Value added tax	308.90	279.90	90.60
(iv) Special tax regimes	201.70	203.30	100.80
(v) Internal excise taxes	30.20	33.50	110.90
(vi) Natural resource tax	178.30	198.20	111.10
(vii) Other domestic taxes and payments on goods and services	36.10	39.50	109.20
NON-TAX REVENUES	26.00	70.30	270.40
(i) Proceeds from property and business activities	...	3.80	...
(ii) Other obligatory payments to the budget	0.80	2.30	278.30
(iii) Fines and sanctions	...	1.20	...
(iv) Other non-tax revenues and administrative payments	22.00	62.70	284.30
(v) Capital income	3.10	0.30	11.10
Balance	78.30	78.30	100.00
Financial assistance (subvention) from the national budget	262.50	262.50	100.00
Mutual settlements from the national budget	5.30	5.30	100.00
TOTAL REVENUES	2,073.70	2,164.10	104.40

... = not available.

[a] Only property tax and excess collection (difference between collected and planned) remain with the municipality. Other revenues are subject to a tax-sharing agreement between the national budget and local budget, as defined in the Law on State Budget for the year.

Source: Ministry of Finance, Republic of Tajikistan.

National and local tax-sharing arrangements are set in the Law on State Budget. Some national taxes fall under tax-sharing arrangements with local budgets in accordance with Article 13 of Law on State Budget of the Republic of Tajikistan. This article stipulates the taxes for sharing on an annual basis, since the Law on State Budget is an annual law.

According to the MOF, municipalities' revenue rate (including tax collection) is on average over 100% of what is planned. Nevertheless, there are municipalities in which revenues do not sufficiently cover expenditures and this trend is increasing. For example, 10 years ago, only five districts in the Sugd region were unable to balance their expenditures, but over time this number rose to 11. In 2021, a total of TJS270 million in subsidies were allocated from the regional budget. Only seven out of 18 subsidized districts in Sugd region had more revenues than expenses.[128]

The local budgets of GBAO, Khatlon region, and nine districts of the DRS present deficits. The total deficit, including subsidies from the State Budget, is forecast to be TJS16.2 million. For 2022, the State Budget allocated TJS1.14 billion as subventions to these local budgets to cover payroll expenditures.[129]

Management of Municipal Financial Resources

***Hukumats* have control of city budget preparation, submission, and execution.** The *hukumats*—comprising the mayors' offices in the cities and the district chairpersons' offices in the districts—develop and approve the norms for local budgetary provisions and establish the general rules for organizing the local budget. They submit a draft annual budget for the next financial year to the relevant *majilis* or people's deputies (Parliament) and prepare and submit the subsequent proposals for amendments and additions as needed. They control the execution of the local budget, including the collection of revenues, and approve the budget execution report for the past financial year. The Law on Public Finance provides a list of participants in the budget process, including the legislature and executive, budget organizations, and public corporations. The public at large is not a participant in the budget process.

The multiyear perspective in fiscal planning and budgeting has not yet taken root. The Law on Public Finances has provided clearer guidelines on local expenditure planning and financing, including cost-sharing (Table 21). But the SNGs as well as the national government have not built on these guidelines to develop multiyear financial approaches. The budgets in Tajikistan are adopted only for one year and the quality of budgeting is poor. First, capital expenditures are budgeted without proper regard for their future recurrent expenditures. Second, there are 58 budget organizations including ministries, state committees, committees under the governments, state agencies, and agencies directly reporting to MOF, which causes fragmentation and affects sector-based allocation and expenditure management. As a result, there is a poor linkage between policy and allocation of budget resources.

---

[128] *Sputnik Tajikistan*. 2022. Data on Income of Districts in Sugd Region Has Been Disclosed. 23 February. Available in Russian.

[129] Law of the Republic of Tajikistan on State Budget for 2022.

Table 21: Local Activities and Financing Sources

Activities exclusively financed from local budgets	Joint expenditures of state and local budgets
• Activities of local state executive bodies of state authority • Activities of self-government bodies of towns and villages • Formation and management of communal property • Activities and development of institutions belonging to communal property or under the jurisdiction of local executive bodies of state authority including education, healthcare, culture, sports and physical education, and periodicals • Development of housing and communal services • Local roads construction and maintenance • Landscaping and related activities • Household waste processing • Transport services for population and institutions in communal ownership or under the jurisdiction of local executive bodies of state authority • Local environmental protection • Implementation of targeted local government programs • Servicing and repayment of debt of local executive bodies of state authority • Transfers to population • Election of local government representative bodies • Financing of local executive decisions and other expenses related to issues of localized importance	• State support for industries, construction, agriculture, energy, transport, communications, and road facilities • Law enforcement • Fire safety • Scientific research, experimental design, and design and survey activities that ensure scientific and technological progress • Social protection, education, healthcare, culture, and sports • Protection of nature, protection and reproduction of natural resources, and hydrometeorological activities • Prevention and elimination of consequences of emergency situations and disasters • Development of market infrastructure • Media activities • Financial assistance to other budgets • Other expenses jointly administered by state authorities and administration, local executive bodies of state authority, and self-government bodies of towns and villages

Source: Articles 18 and 19, Law on Public Finances, Republic of Tajikistan.

Creditworthiness

No creditworthiness assessment has been conducted for the municipalities in Tajikistan. Access to financing is a major hurdle to sustainable urban development. Already under pressure, infrastructure and basic services (transport, solid waste management, and water and sanitation) need to be expanded significantly to adequately serve the growing population. Traditional sources of financing from the central government and international financial institutions (IFIs) will not be nearly sufficient to meet the demand. Municipalities will have to seek other sources of long-term financing such as through public–private partnerships (PPPs), for which a law was adopted in 2012.[130] However, to attract investments from private sources, municipalities need to first be creditworthy.

Municipal borrowing capacity is limited to borrowing from the national budget. Currently, municipalities can borrow money in the form of budgetary loans from the state budget only. To increase the creditworthiness of local municipalities and attract investments from sources other than the state budget, the World Bank through the International Development Association tried to set up the Communal Services Development Fund in 2015 to address the growing urban infrastructure needs in water and sanitation and transport and logistics via the anticipated Communal Services Development Fund Project.[131] However, because of changes in financing terms, the project was canceled at Tajikistan's request.[132]

There is no mechanism for municipalities to borrow from outside. Municipal companies, i.e., municipal branches of water, waste, and airport utilities, were able to borrow from IFIs and bilateral partners under certain conditions: a financier provides a loan to the municipal company under sovereign guarantee, and the municipality commits to support the investment project by signing a contractual municipal support agreement with the financier. This agreement includes a general commitment to support the project and facilitate key decisions (such as tariff adjustments). However, according to the MOF, only the ministry will be able to borrow under the new legislation, which excludes municipalities or SUEs.[133]

---

[130] Commonwealth of Independent States (CIS) Legislation. Law of the Republic of Tajikistan Public–Private Partnership Adopted 28 December 2012. No. 907.

[131] World Bank. 2015. *Tajikistan - Communal Services Development Fund Project. Resettlement Policy Framework.* Washington, DC.

[132] Grant financing of 100% was changed to a 100% loan.

[133] Consultation with MOF.

Government Policies and External Assistance

3.1 Government Policies

An urbanization policy framework is emerging. Although no document provides an overall and cohesive vision of urbanization, the Government of Tajikistan has issued several urbanization-related policy and regulatory documents in the past 6 years. These include:

- National Development Strategy of the Republic of Tajikistan for the period up to 2030 (NDS 2030), issued in 2016;
- Strategy for Development of the Construction Industry of the Republic of Tajikistan for the period up to 2030, issued in 2022;
- Housing Code of the Republic of Tajikistan, which came into force in September 2022; and
- Government Resolution No. 335, on construction of at least five-story residential buildings in administrative centers of cities and districts of the Republic of Tajikistan, issued in 2018.

National Development Strategy 2030

The NDS 2030 is Tajikistan's first strategic policy for national development. It replaces the previous five-year programs under the Poverty Reduction Strategy Papers that focused on meeting the population's basic and immediate needs after the civil war. The NDS considers urbanization enabling outcomes such as establishing the institutional foundations for urban development through a sound land policy, strengthening the right of ownership, and improving housing and infrastructure services.

The strategy highlights the need for accelerated urbanization. It also emphasizes the need to transition to "large-scale housing construction, faster growth of investments in the community-based, social, and road infrastructure and sets as a priority the urbanization and promotion of urban processes in the regions, including in small towns."[134] The following measures are envisaged for the promotion of urban development processes:

- development of the institutional framework for further urbanization, including on urban development planning, housing and land policy, and streamlining and registration of land and property ownership rights;

---

[134] Footnote 8, Chapter 3.2.

- development of housing market and promotion of residential and commercial real estate and infrastructure in urban areas;
- development of small towns as centers of innovative activity;
- improvement of housing and communal services in settlements (water supply, sewerage, gas, heat, electricity supply, collection and disposal of household waste), which is expected to create new jobs, address environmental problems, and increase the competitiveness of the regions; and
- promotion of modern retail networks and provision of consumer services.

In the area of developing territorial and industrial clusters and economic corridors, the NDS will

- create conditions for the development of energy, industrial, transport and logistics, food, and education clusters in regions, which will serve as integral elements of the existing global and regional value chains and improve competitiveness of the national economy;
- accelerate the development of free economic zones and new industrial territories; and
- build the capacity of economic corridors that connect the regions of Tajikistan with Afghanistan, Central Asian countries, India, the Middle East, Pakistan, the PRC, the Russian Federation, Southeast Asia, and other regions.

To spatially expand the labor market, the NDS will

- develop mechanisms to stimulate sustainable development initiatives by the population and various social groups and organizations at the district, town, and village levels;
- diversify economic activities in the regions; and
- expand short-term employment programs, considering the needs and interests of men and women, youth, persons with disabilities, and other social groups.

Some inconsistencies can be observed in the development strategy benchmarks. According to the benchmarks it provides, the NDS foresees a consistent increase in the GDP contribution of the industrial sector between 2020 and 2030 and a decline in that of the services sector (excluding construction) during the period (Table 22). The decline in the services sector is striking as it is a predominantly urban sector, while the industrial business model require larger tracts of land at low prices, which are usually not found in urban areas. The services sector figures also appear inaccurate, with the contribution of the "services sector including construction" projected to be consistently lower than the contribution of the "services sector excluding construction."[135] Incidentally, the figures on the row "including construction" match the figures presented in the Strategy for the Development of the Construction Industry on the contribution of the construction industry alone to GDP.

Table 22: National Development Strategy Benchmarks

Benchmarks (Unit of Measurement)	Baseline 2015	Industrial Scenario			Industrial Innovative Scenario		
		2020	2025	2030	2020	2025	2030
Population: end of year (1,000 people)	8,547.4 (prior to 1 January 2016)	9,500.0	10,490.0	11,580.0	9,500.0	10,490.0	11,580.0
GDP per capita (TJS)	5,663.0	8,430.0	12,297.0	17,754.0	8,869.0	14,302.0	23,131.0
Average real GDP growth per year (%)	6.0	6.7	6.9	7.8	7.5	8.9	9.6
			6–7.0			8–9.0	
Ratio of gross domestic savings to GDP (%)	18.0	22.0	26.0	28.0	30.0	35.0	40.0
Share of private investment in GDP (%)	5.0	10.0	15.0	18.0	12.0	20.0	25.0
Share of industry in GDP (%)	12.3	12.5–13.2	16.0	20–20.5	13–13.5	16–16.5	20–21.0
Extractive industry (%)	...	11–12.0	11–11.5	9–10.0	11–11.5	10–10.5	8–9.0
Processing industry (%)	...	72–74.0	74–75.0	75.5–76.0	73–74.0	75–76.0	78–78.5
Production and distribution of gas, water, and energy (%)	...	15–16.0	14– 14.5	14–14.5	15–15.5	14–14.5	13–13.5
Share of agriculture in GDP (%)	23.3	21.0	20.1	19–19.5	19.5–20.5	18–18.5	17–18
Share of services in GDP (excluding construction) (%)	...	37–37.5	34–34.5	28.5–29.5	38–38.5	25–255.0	30–30.6
Share of services in GDP (including construction) (%)	...	16–16.5	17–17.6	18.5–19.5	16–16.5	18–18.5	19.2–20.2
Net indirect taxes in GDP (%)	13.2	12.6	12.5	12.5	12.3	12.0	12.0

... = not available, GDP = gross domestic product, TJS = Tajikistan somoni.

Note: Entries on the second row of the average real GDP growth per capita for the industrial and industrial innovative scenarios represent the range of the average growth for each scenario during the whole period.

Source: Ministry of Economic Development and Trade of the Republic of Tajikistan. 2016. *National Development Strategy of the Republic of Tajikistan for the Period Up to 2030*. Dushanbe.

Construction Industry Strategy

The Strategy for the Development of the Construction Industry for the period up to 2030 aims to increase the potential of the industry. Issued in April 2022, it defines aspects of the state policy on urban development, emphasizing among others the following goals:

---

[135] This data issue is reflected in both Russian and English versions of the document.

- better state control of the use of land through improved regulatory framework and stronger coordination between state administration and local government;
- balanced development of territorial units and settlements;
- improved livability and environmental conditions, including better public spaces, the development of transport infrastructure including transport hubs, improved waste management with separate collection and regional waste processing complexes, and the preservation and enhanced use of historical buildings;
- digitalization, including development of information modeling in urban planning documentation and the optimization of the methodology for maintaining the state urban planning cadastre; and
- improved public awareness of the planned changes.

Construction is a key growth industry. The share of the construction industry in Tajikistan's GDP was around 16% in 2020. It is expected to reach 19.5% in 2030 (footnote 13). This is remarkable, considering that in neighboring Uzbekistan, the construction industry contributed only 6.5% to GDP in 2019 (footnote 34). The strategy foresees an increase of no less than 20% until 2030 in the average number of people employed annually in construction, which in 2020 was around 109,000. It acknowledges that an increase in the number of construction organizations will lead to an increase in competitiveness and the GDP. In support of this, the state plans to improve the investment environment for foreign and domestic investors and introduce PPP mechanisms.

The urban planning system needs reforms. The process of updating general plans for Tajikistan cities and settlements started in 2005. As of 2022, 65 urban and district centers have updated or developed their general plans. Updates were completed in Kulob in 2008, Khujand in 2010, Bokhtar in 2011, and Dushanbe in 2017.[136] Recognizing that "the system of territorial planning and urban design does not fully meet modern requirements" (footnote 13), the construction industry strategy advocates (i) the introduction of amendments to enhance the Urban Planning Code and (ii) the development of a systematic approach, including tools and methods, to address the implications of the population density increase with the construction of new mid-rise buildings in core areas.[137] Improvements in the building and construction permitting process are also needed to raise the ranking of Tajikistan in the Doing Business Index as well as to strengthen compliance by the construction industry and population to the state's territorial and strategic plans. According to the strategy, zoning regulations will be introduced and made more adaptive to the rapidly mounting physical, demographic, and socioeconomic challenges, including the risks associated with climate change.

---

[136] This urban assessment has no access to the general plans.
[137] This report refers to buildings of 5–9 stories as mid-rise, although in policy documents of the Government of Tajikistan they are referred to as high-rise.

Housing Code

The new Housing Code of the Republic of Tajikistan may be an important stepping stone to transition the country to market-oriented urban development. The Housing Code of 1997, a legacy of the Soviet system, did match the regulatory needs emerging from the wave of privatization that started in 1992. There had been various attempts to update it, but the 1997 law remained in force until recently. After 13 years of discussions, the new Housing Code finally came into effect on 1 September 2022.

The new Housing Code introduces market concepts and terminology. Article 4 introduces concepts such as "residential premises," "residential building," "residential house," "apartment building," "apartment," "room," "housing stock," "total area of the apartment," "technical passport of a residential building," "common property of an apartment building," "social rent," "adjacent territory," "management organization," "homeowners' association," and "housing cooperative," which were not included in the previous code.[138] The introduction of these concepts is expected to prepare the ground for the development of the housing market.

Clarifying roles should be an essential objective of the Housing Code. It is not known at this point if under the new Housing Code state agencies in the field of housing construction retain the same competences or if the Code establishes a new, market-fitting institutional set-up.

Resolution 335: On Construction of At Least Five-Story Residential Buildings

The resolution promotes compact growth, but this needs to be organized. In 2018, the president signed Government Resolution 335 requiring residential buildings in administrative centers of cities and districts to be at least five stories. The resolution aims to establish a rational and effective use of land to prevent the reduction of arable land and prohibit its transformation into buildable land without grounds. It mandated the CAC, together with relevant ministries and departments, executive bodies of state authority in GBAO, regions, Dushanbe, cities, and districts, to take necessary measures to implement the resolution, including adjustments to the urban planning documentation (footnote 79).

---

[138] The New Housing Code of the Republic of Tajikistan consists of 8 sections, 18 chapters, and 141 articles, expounding on and providing the legal basis for key subject matters such as property rights to housing, housing stock management, public housing stock, housing cooperative, renting housing, and payments and benefits in the housing sector.

3.2 External Assistance

ADB's Lending and Technical Assistance Program

ADB is the country's largest multilateral development partner. Since 1998, ADB has committed 184 public sector loans, grants, and technical assistance totaling $2.48 billion to Tajikistan (Table 23).[139] Cumulative loan and grant disbursements to Tajikistan amount to $1.58 billion. These were financed by concessional ordinary capital resources, the Asian Development Fund, and other special funds. ADB's ongoing sovereign portfolio in Tajikistan includes 3 loans and 21 grants worth $943.2 million.[140]

Other Development Partners

World Bank Group. Tajikistan joined the World Bank in 1993 and the International Development Association in 1994. Since then, the World Bank has provided over $2.44 billion in grants, credits, and trust. Its Country Partnership Framework for 2019–2023 mentions efforts to complement Tajikistan's remittance-financed, import-reliant economic model with a focus on boosting private sector development and exports. Its country partnership priorities were recently realigned to address the immediate socioeconomic challenges resulting from the COVID-19 pandemic, financing of which totaled $57.5 million. These investments helped strengthen healthcare capacity, supported vulnerable households with cash transfers, and provided Tajikistan with internationally approved COVID-19 vaccines.

European Bank for Reconstruction and Development. As of end-2022, the EBRD had supported 152 projects, cumulatively amounting to €916 million (€551 million current portfolio), with 13% private sector share. In Tajikistan, the EBRD focuses on stabilizing and rebuilding trust in the banking sector; developing private enterprises and agribusiness; improving the availability, reliability, and quality of municipal services; and improving the quality of energy supply, regulation, and energy efficiency. Its latest country strategy for Tajikistan, adopted in 2020, set the EBRD's 2020–2025 priorities as addressing issues related to a volatile macroeconomic environment, a challenging business climate, and vulnerability to climate change. Priorities will aim to improve Tajikistan's infrastructure, its regional connectivity, and employment opportunities.

Japan International Cooperation Agency (JICA). JICA began its technical cooperation with Tajikistan in 1993. It established an office in-country in 2006 as a branch of the JICA Uzbekistan Office. Since then, various grant financial assistance and technical cooperation projects have been implemented, aiming to improve living standards in Tajikistan for sectors such as agriculture and rural development, water supply, health, and transport. JICA's programs have included improvement of water supply, maternal and child health, poverty reduction by agricultural and industrial development, energy, and transport.

Select projects and activities of other development partners are provided in Appendix 2.

---

[139] ADB. Tajikistan: Cumulative Commitments.

[140] Sovereign portfolio comprises loans, grants, equity investment, and sovereign guarantee committed and not financially closed.

Table 23: ADB Cumulative Commitments
(as of April 2023)

Sector	No. of Projects	Total Amount ($ million)	% of Total Amount	COVID-19 Response ($ million)
Project and Technical Assistance	184.00	2,480.00	99.20	80.45
Agriculture, Natural Resources, and Rural Development	42.00	269.70	10.87	
Education	13.00	76.38	3.31	
Energy	22.00	594.83	23.99	
Finance	16.00	154.25	6.22	0.63
Health	10.00	72.42	2.92	29.24
Industry and Trade	6.00	25.11	1.01	0.21
Information and Communication Technology	...	0.32	0.01	0.07
Multisector	7.00	53.83	2.17	
Public Sector Management	23.00	256.41	10.34	50.30
Transport	34.00	825.07	33.26	
Water and Other Urban Infrastructure and Services	8.00	95.33	3.84	
Trade and Supply Chain Finance Program	147.00	18.15	0.80	1.59
Finance	78.00	9.87	0.43	1.59
Industry and Trade	69.00	8.28	0.36	
Total	322.00	2,275.90	100.00	82.04

– = nil, ADB = Asian Development Bank, COVID-19 = coronavirus disease, DMC = developing member country.

Notes:

(i) This table summarizes all forms of ADB cumulative commitments to the Republic of Tajikistan. Commitment refers to financing approved by the ADB Board of Directors or Management for which the legal agreement has been signed by the borrower, recipient, or the investee company.

(ii) Projects include loans and grants. Grants and technical assistance include ADB-administered cofinancing. From 2020, financing for technical assistance projects with regional coverage (e.g., Central and West Asia) is distributed to specific DMCs where breakdown is available.

(iii) Sector represents primary sector assisted. Trade and supply chain finance programs represent short-term ADB commitments from private sector programs with maturity of less than 365 days.

(iv) Numbers may not sum precisely because of rounding.

Source: ADB. Tajikistan: Cumulative Commitments.

Development Challenges and Priorities

4.1 Urban Sector Problems

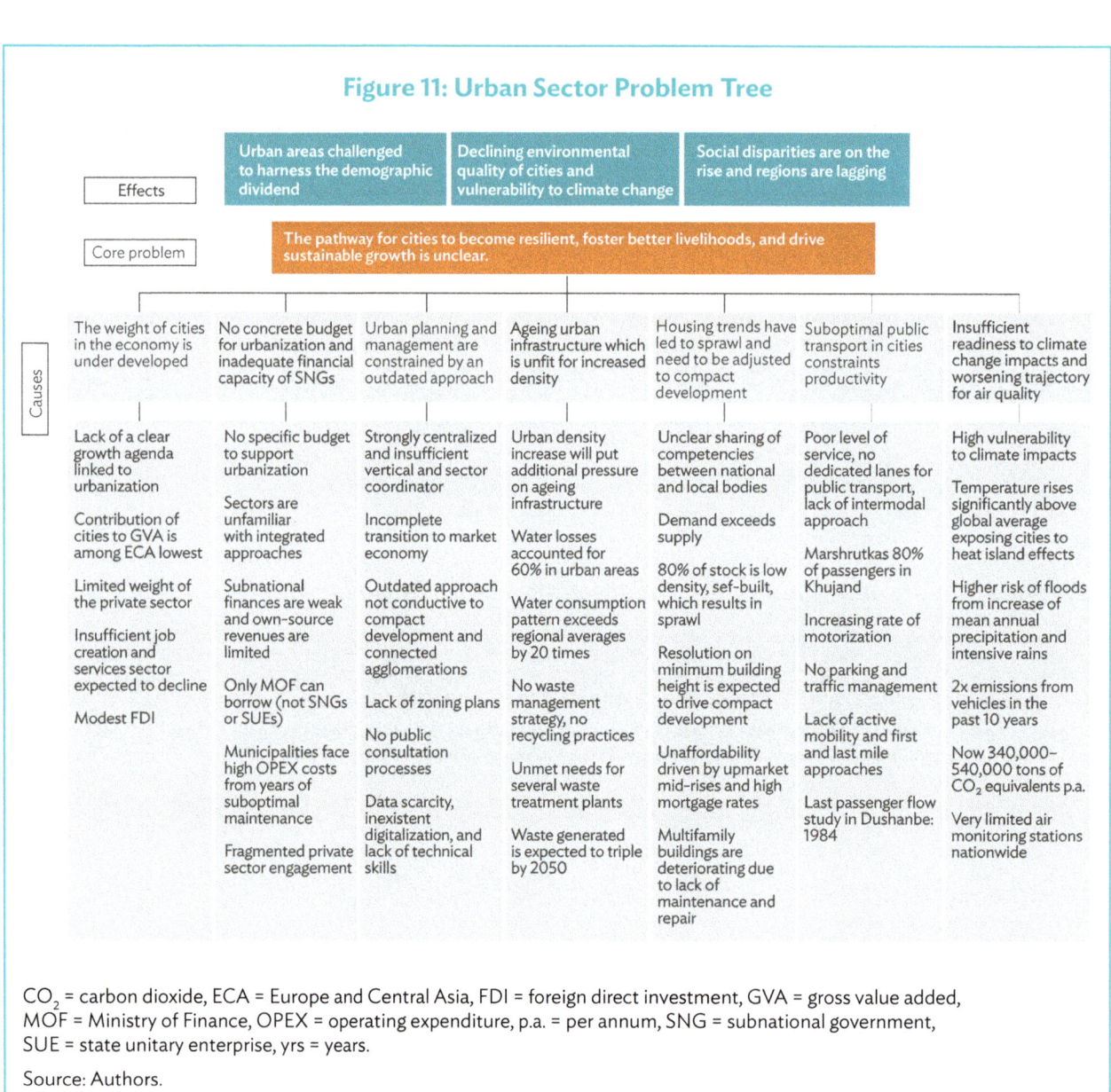

Figure 11: Urban Sector Problem Tree

CO_2 = carbon dioxide, ECA = Europe and Central Asia, FDI = foreign direct investment, GVA = gross value added, MOF = Ministry of Finance, OPEX = operating expenditure, p.a. = per annum, SNG = subnational government, SUE = state unitary enterprise, yrs = years.

Source: Authors.

4.2 Causes

A host of complex, interrelated causes underlie the multifaceted urban sector problems of Tajikistan (Figure 11).

The important role of cities in the economy is underdeveloped. The level of foreign investment, aggregating $346 million in 2019 (76% from the PRC) is considered modest.[141] The finance sector traditionally has been viewed as a weak segment of Tajikistan's economy, and domestic credit to the private sector accounted for only 12.3% of GDP in 2017.[142] Urban gross value added to GDP growth is among the lowest in Europe and Central Asia, at around 50%.[143] Economic activity is characterized by limited private sector contribution and insufficient productivity and job creation, resulting in an estimated 200,000 additional job seekers annually.[144] It is hampered by the lack of a clear growth agenda linked to urbanization and may be compounded by an expected decline of the services sector by 7% in 2030 (footnote 8, p. 91).

The government has no specific budget for urbanization, and the financial capacity of subnational governments is inadequate. The MOF has no dedicated budget to support urbanization, which is expected to be covered by sector budgets that are not familiar with integrated approaches. Subnational finances are weak and own-source revenues are limited. Property tax is the only source assigned to the local level. The foundations for land-based cost recovery do not exist. According to new legislation, only the MOF can borrow (not municipalities or SUEs).[145] Municipalities face high operating costs from years of suboptimal asset maintenance. Engagement of the private sector in urban development is fragmented, and the strategic perspective of its role in urbanization is not apparent.

Urban planning and management are constrained by an outdated approach. A legacy of the Soviet period, the current urban planning process in Tajikistan is strongly centralized. The outdated spatial approach is dominated by segregated land use, large but inaccessible public spaces, and wide avenues that prioritize vehicles and not pedestrians. There is no agglomeration approach as plans are constrained by municipal administrative boundaries. General plan approaches are disconnected from the needs of compact urban development. Plans can be produced only by the Dushanbe-based SUE *Shahrofar* under the structure of the CAC.[146] The fact that only one entity can produce and update the high number of general plans and detailed plans required by the transition to a compact pattern may result in a bottleneck. Coordination between the central level and municipalities and between sectors is inadequate, and the lack of urban planners at the central and municipal

---

[141] BTI Transformation Index. 2022. Tajikistan Country Report.
[142] ADB. 2021. *Country Partnership Strategy: Tajikistan, 2021–2025—Improving the Quality of Growth*. Manila.
[143] P. Restrepo Cadavid et al. 2017. *Cities in Europe and Central Asia. A Shifting Story of Urban Growth and Decline*. Washington, DC: World Bank Group.
[144] Consultation with the Institute of Economics and Demography of the Academy of Sciences.
[145] Consultation with MOF.
[146] JSC Shahrofar.

levels is a key barrier.¹⁴⁷ There is no stakeholder input or public consultation in urban planning. The creation of an urban land market is mentioned by the NDS; however, the transition from planned to market economy in urban development is largely incomplete. The ownership of land remains with the state, and there are no zoning maps available, hence, construction permits are issued largely on a case-by-case basis. Digitalization is almost nonexistent, the scarce data is only at a macro level, and access to information is difficult, hampering accurate policymaking and investment decisions.

Aging infrastructure and services will be unable to meet the demands posed by increased urbanization. The increase in demand for urban housing and associated urban infrastructure and services are significant challenges for municipal governments. Water supply pipelines are aging, and water losses reach 60% in urban areas. The water consumption pattern exceeds the subregional and regional averages by over 20 times, which puts the system under significant stress. In Bokhtar, the water supply system was designed for 50,000 persons and it now serves 400,000.¹⁴⁸ Waste management is a crucial sector, as waste generated is expected to triple by 2050. However, currently, there is no solid waste management strategy and no recycling practices, only an outdated overall approach with unmet needs for several waste treatment plants.¹⁴⁹

Housing trends have led to sprawl and need to be adjusted to compact development. A study released by the United Nations Economic Commission for Europe (UNECE) a decade ago identified housing as a largely unfunded mandate, with an unclear sharing of competencies between national and local bodies (footnote 26). The lack of clarity is perceived to have not been completely addressed. Land and housing policy has historically favored self-built units, which today account for about 80% of all the housing stock. This has resulted in a sprawling spatial pattern. The requirement for all new residential buildings in core urban areas to have at least five stories is intended to reduce land consumption. However, it is unclear if Resolution 335 will change the overall sprawling trend. The new mid-rise buildings are priced as upmarket solutions, and in Dushanbe, the price per square meter in core areas is twice as high as in peri-urban areas. As demand for housing exceeds supply and the mortgage market is inaccessible for most of the population, this is likely to drive homebuyers to peri-urban areas, where Resolution 335 may not apply. Multifamily residential buildings are deteriorating due to the lack of maintenance and repair. Although the Law on Apartment Building Maintenance and Homeowner Associations contains provisions on the management of common areas, sitting tenants still do not perceive that they are responsible for housing management. The importance of maintenance as a precondition for keeping the value of the building is still barely understood.¹⁵⁰

Suboptimal public transport in cities restricts productivity. Public transport, essential for compact urban development, is underdeveloped. The rate of motorization is increasing, with room to expand as Tajikistan has only one-third of

---

[147] Consultations with the CAC.
[148] Consultation with the Bokhtar municipal government.
[149] Consultation with the Committee on Environment Protection.
[150] Habitat for Humanity. 2013. *Housing Review 2013*. Vienna.

the number of vehicles registered in the Kyrgyz Republic and one-eighth of that in Kazakhstan. This is likely to result in increased congestion which will have negative consequences for productivity. *Marshrutkas* carry 80% of passengers in Khujand where approximately 20,000 daily trips take place from the agglomeration to central city.[151] The concept of mobility is still to be grasped in planning and investment decision-making. Public transport is hampered in Tajikistan's main cities by the lack of dedicated lanes and poor service level, no active mobility policy or last-mile approach to inter-modality, lack of transport data, no parking management strategy, and chaotic and an undermaintained secondary and tertiary road network, which will increasingly make it difficult to access areas with new mid-rise residential buildings.

Insufficient readiness to climate change impacts in cities and worsening trajectory of air quality. Tajikistan is highly vulnerable to climate impacts. In 2021, it was ranked 140th by the Notre Dame Global Adaptation Initiative's Country Index out of 182 countries when it comes to climate change readiness (footnote 9). The average seasonal maximum temperature has increased by 1°C and temperature rises are projected significantly above the global average. Cities will be more exposed to heat island effects. The mean annual precipitation has increased, and rains have become intensive, which means that the risk of floods is higher. This is especially relevant for compact urban patterns which should be designed so they are ready to respond to heat island effects and floods, which will ensure business continuity and livability standards. The air quality of cities can be currently considered moderate, but it is worsening. Emissions from vehicles have doubled in the past decade (footnote 85). In Dushanbe, negative contributors are a cement factory and a coal power and heat plant. In general, information on air quality is limited as there are only 16 air quality monitoring stations nationwide, six of them in Dushanbe.

4.3 Priority Issues

Economy: Urban areas will be challenged to harness the demographic dividend.

The demographic dividend is a unique window of opportunity. The NDS identifies the expected growth of the working-age population as an opportunity to drive economic growth. The national population will increase by 1.5 million by 2030, and in the next 15 years, the population aged between 15 and 64 years old will reach 60% of the total. While the NDS considers working-age population growth as a "window of opportunity," it acknowledges that if efforts are not undertaken, it could turn into a "window of demographic threat" (footnote 8).

Tajikistan is yet to urbanize. While the urbanization rate is projected to reach 32% in 2030, it will remain the lowest in Central Asia. The fact that urbanization is yet to happen in Tajikistan amplifies the likelihood of the demographic opportunity resulting in the frequently positive correlation between a higher degree of urbanization and

---

[151] Consultation with Khujand municipal government.

improved social and economic conditions. However, this is not a given. Unresolved challenges may lock in cities to unproductive trajectories and spatial patterns that contribute to letting the urbanization opportunity slip away, unfulfilled. Congested roads, pollution, precarious housing, limited access to services, and development in areas exposed to extreme weather events can be considered early warning signs.

Urban employment is required to capitalize on the demographic dividend. A study by the World Bank concluded that urban sectors are almost three times more productive than the rural sectors in Tajikistan.[152] Urban sector jobs will be more efficient in capturing the demographic dividend and thus become an alternative to outmigration for the working-age population, including women. The connection between urbanization and the demographic dividend is well established in the NDS, which acknowledges that urbanization will drive the increase in productivity needed to prevent a decline in the standard of living of the growing population.

Urbanization, economic development, and private sector activity are insufficiently linked. Without a specific strategy that links economic development to urbanization, cities will be challenged to be the main generators of employment that the demographic pyramid demands. The share of private investment in GDP has been much lower than regional comparators (footnote 39). The private sector has been central in creating opportunities for employment in urbanizing countries, however, its current weight in key urban sectors such as real estate development, construction, and tourism is limited. The development of a housing market, the promotion of residential and commercial real estate, and the use of public–private partnership mechanisms in housing are acknowledged as objectives of the NDS.

Environment: The environmental quality and disaster vulnerability of cities are a growing concern.

Inadequate assessment and incorporation of disaster risks in urban development planning increases vulnerability—and this is likely to be exacerbated by climate change. Tajikistan is exposed to various hazards, including earthquakes, mudflows, landslides, and avalanches, and the chances of these hazards causing disasters are high, particularly in those associated with climate change. In addition to the population's lack of adaptive capacity, no government agency is currently directly responsible for disaster management and risk mitigation. Disaster risk reduction and climate change adaptation are still not systematically addressed in urban plans and sectoral strategies (footnote 9). Risk mapping is not sufficiently incorporated in land use planning, aggravating vulnerability and disaster impacts in areas where there is a concentration of population and assets in vulnerable locations. The lack of a systematic approach to green areas in urban contexts and poor data availability on green cover and open spaces lower the ability of Tajikistan's cities to reduce heat island effects, an important aspect of compact urban development.

---

[152] In 2013, the estimated urban to rural gross value added was 2.45, compared to an urban to rural population ratio of 0.36. See: World Bank. 2023. Project Information Document (PID). Dushanbe Sustainable Urban Development Project (P179630).

Sewerage network deficiencies contribute to environmental degradation.
Sewerage services are available to about 70% of the population in Dushanbe, according to the SUE *Dushanbevodokanal*, while the remainder, particularly those in newly developed areas, uses septic tanks. The sewerage system is characterized by the ingress of groundwater, and overflows to water bodies and land. The wastewater treatment plant functions poorly, with only marginal treatment achieved. Various municipalities in other cities have also identified inadequate sewerage systems as a key issue. In Bokhtar, this is compounded by the recurrence of floods. Nearly 80% of Tajikistan's average annual loss from floods, estimated at $60.8 million, is borne by Khatlon, the region where Bokhtar is (footnote 9).

Despite investments in solid waste management, key challenges remain. There is no solid waste management policy at the national level. In larger cities, insufficient collection points and waste management services are a main challenge, and it is not uncommon for solid waste to lay in the open, uncollected for days. This situation will be compounded by urban growth. Policies for the reduction of consumption are in the infancy stages and waste recycling is marginal.[153] The capacity of municipal waste collection companies is minimal. In Dushanbe, the landfill site does not meet international standards and solid waste disposal and management practices are outdated.[154] According to the Committee on Environment Protection, one solid waste treatment plant is needed in every region including the Dushanbe area.[155]

The inadequate approach to urban mobility limits productivity and contributes to deteriorating air quality in cities. Privately run *marshrutkas* dominate the modal split in large cities. These minivans compete with buses and trolleys operated by state-owned enterprises which are hampered by poor bus network planning, dearth of data, no prioritization in traffic, deficient revenue streams, and dependence on operational subsidies. The disconnection between urban land use and transport planning negatively affects the connectivity between urban cores and peri-urban areas. First and last-mile approaches are not considered, and there are no incentives for non-motorized mobility, which aggravates road safety issues. New mid-rise buildings sit on poorly designed streets and are being built without a parking management strategy. The second- and third-level road networks are not well maintained and connectivity across urban gaps, for example, rivers and rail tracks, is suboptimal. These aspects are contributing to increasing congestion and putting cities on a pathway of deteriorating air quality, with emissions from vehicles doubling in the past decade (footnote 85). Cars and trucks are responsible for more than 70% of harmful emissions, which indicates that steps must be taken in public transport to mitigate a worsening trajectory.[156]

---

[153] These policies are embodied in the Green Economy Development Strategy for 2023–2037, approved by the government in September 2022.
[154] EBRD. 2022. *Dushanbe Green City Action Plan: Summary Presentation to ADB*. July.
[155] Consultation with the Committee on Environment Protection.
[156] Committee for Environment Protection under the Government of the Republic of Tajikistan. 2018. *Tajikistan Environment and Ecological Report. Dushanbe* (available in hard copy only).

Equity: Social disparities are on the rise and regions are lagging.

Tourism can contribute to reduce regional imbalances. This is one of the objectives of the CAREC Tourism Strategy 2030.[157] At the national level, the promotion of greater economic integration within Central Asia through the development of economic corridors supported by adequate road infrastructure, logistics facilities, and land development will enable the availability of tourism services, while contributing to reducing inequality in access to basic services and disparity in poverty rates across regions.[158] At an urban level, tapping the tourism potential of Dushanbe and other cities with tourism assets such as Khujand, Kulob, Hissor, and Bokhtar requires improvement of tourism infrastructure facilities, urban development interventions in safe and comfortable transport, and attractive urban design in areas with potential for year-round activities. Tourism institutional capacity building and a tourism development plan that incorporates a gender perspective will provide an opportunity to revert the fact that about 69% of working-age women are not working for pay, and women's contribution to gross national income is 4.5 times less than that of men.[159]

Increasing social disparities may exacerbate housing poverty. In 2021, Tajikistan had a housing stock of 1.23 million units, which is equivalent to 163 dwellings per 1,000 inhabitants, the lowest of all countries in the Europe and Central Asia region (footnote 39). There is little information on both supply and demand in the housing sector, and updated information on the previously mentioned benchmark is not available. This impedes having an accurate picture of the extent of housing poverty and trends. The NDS identifies an increase in and improvement of housing provisions by 2030 as long-term policy objectives. Improved housing provisions will consist of better-quality new construction and the renovation of existing residential properties in suboptimal condition. However, the NDS only has one housing benchmark—an increase in residential floor space per capita to 17 m^2 in 2030, up from 12 m^2 in 2015—which may be insufficient to guide downstream action planning. The NDS recognizes that policy adjustment is required in the new mid-rise construction initiative as only families with the highest income can benefit from it. The development of mortgage lending standards is particularly relevant as are an integrated operational plan for compact urban development and a housing strategy.

The lack of public consultation in urban planning and development erodes the potential of implementing change. Stakeholder participation in the preparation of urban plans and in investment project identification is nonexistent.[160] Civic actors are also excluded from performance monitoring. A World Bank report indicated eroding civil trust and declining state legitimacy due to limited government responsiveness to local concerns (footnote 38). Strong central control has disempowered local

---

[157] CAREC and ADB. 2020. *CAREC Tourism Strategy 2030*. Manila.
[158] For example, the poverty rate is 17% in Sugd and 32% in Khatlon, despite the decline in poverty rates by 10% across 2012–2018. Source: World Bank. 2019. *Poverty in Tajikistan*.
[159] World Bank. 2021. *Tajikistan Country Gender Assessment*. Washington, DC.
[160] For more details, see section on Urban Planning and Management, p. 42.

governments and communities and thereby failed to mobilize local support for the government. The engagement of civil society is further constrained by the limited financing scope available to NGOs.

The priority issues are summarized in Table 24.

Table 24: Summary of Priority Issues

Economy	Environment	Equity
Urban areas will be challenged to harness the demographic dividend.	**The environmental quality and disaster vulnerability of cities are a growing concern.**	**Social disparities are on the rise and regions are lagging.**
The demographic dividend provides a unique window of opportunity.	Inadequate assessment and incorporation of disaster risks in urban development planning increases vulnerability—and this is likely to be exacerbated by climate change.	Access to opportunities and services is unequal across regions.
Tajikistan is yet to urbanize.		Increasing social disparities may exacerbate housing poverty.
Urban employment is required to benefit from the demographic dividend.	Sewerage network deficiencies contribute to environmental degradation.	The lack of public consultation in urban planning and development erodes the feasibility of government programs and initiatives.
Urbanization, economic growth, and private sector development are insufficiently linked.	Despite investments in solid waste management, key challenges remain.	
	The inadequate approach to urban mobility limits productivity and contributes to deteriorating air quality in cities.	

Source: Authors.

4.4 Core Problem

The core problem of Tajikistan's urban sector can be summarized as follows:

> **The pathway for cities to become resilient, foster better livelihoods, and drive sustainable growth is unclear.**

Tajikistan is at a key moment for placing urbanization at the center of its growth agenda. The NDS describes the demographic dividend in the next decade as a moment of opportunity for Tajikistan. The increase in population will require new jobs, and urban sectors are significantly more productive than rural sectors. The low urbanization rate should motivate focal urban state agencies (Table 25) to steer urban development so that it elevates the quality of growth and fosters better livelihoods and more productive economic activities in cities. Shifting the source of growth to efficiency and productivity gains and private investment mobilization is vital (footnote 38).

Table 25: State Agencies Responsible for Urban Development

Sector	Planning	Execution
Water and Sewerage[a]	Committee on Architecture and Construction and municipal departments of architecture and construction	Relevant municipal water companies SUE *Khojagii Manziliyu Kommunali* (KMK)[b]
Waste		SUE *Khojagii Manziliyu Kommunali* (KMK)
Transport		Public and private transportation companies
Roads		Relevant municipal department for road construction
Electricity		Local distribution networks of *Barqi Tojik* (Tajikistan Energy Holding)

[a] Including stormwater drainage mostly in large cities.
[b] State-owned holding company responsible for waste collection and water supply and sanitation.
Source: Authors.

Elevating the quality of growth through urbanization will require a clear pathway. The requirement for all new buildings in core urban areas to be mid-rise is a step in the direction of compact development. Implementing this directive will enable a considerable shift in the spatial pattern of cities away from the sprawling pattern generated by the construction of single-family units. The shift is in the right direction, but orderly compact growth will not happen spontaneously. Fulfilling the role of urbanization as a driver of quality growth requires an operational guide. Policy reforms are imperative: at the national level, through a territorial strategy that establishes a system of cities and informs spatial development and investments for a land-linked economy; and at the city level, through an integrated approach to compact urban development in the core areas of the largest cities (Dushanbe, Khujand, Bokhtar, and Kulob) with upgrades in basic infrastructure and transport and updates in land use planning. Urban planning and management need to be reformed to support the shift to land-linked, compact spatial development; and tapping the private sector requires an enabling environment and firm regulations.

Making Cities in Tajikistan More Livable

Urban development scenarios help categorize indicative actions in the short, medium, and long term. The actions are (i) relevant to the aims of this national urban assessment, (ii) aligned with the overall objective of ADB's Country Partnership Strategy with Tajikistan to elevate the country's quality of growth through, among others, better livelihoods and more livable cities in a land-linked economy (footnote 142); and (iii) supportive of ADB Strategy 2030's Operational Priority 4: Making Cities More Livable, which is subdivided into improving services in urban areas, strengthening urban planning and financial sustainability, and enhancing urban environment and climate resilience.[161] The urban development scenarios are not formulated as alternatives to each other but as an incremental set of development futures that will evolve as Tajikistan makes policy choices to harness opportunities and its comparative advantages.

5.1 Short Term

The short-term scenario (1–5 years) responds to key trends to set the pathway for a futuristic urban development model. Actions, overall, will leverage the demographic dividend and contribute to activating the urban economy envisioned by the NDS 2030.

Mainstreaming urbanization into the growth agenda requires a holistic policy package designed to develop urban economies and create jobs. The objectives should be in correspondence with spatial planning at the national and functional urban area (FUA) levels.[162] Policies and investments will jump-start the trajectory to a land-linked economy and the sustainable consumption of land in order for cities to develop in a more livable, resilient, and equitable manner in the context of population growth and the transition to market-oriented urban development.

By establishing a system of cities, national-level planning will contribute to the trajectory toward equitable access to services across regions for economic opportunities and improved conditions for life. Economic development policies should be closely linked to policies pertaining to the spatial dimension such as the connectivity between lagging regions and cities where services and opportunities tend to be increasingly concentrated. To capitalize on this, the main urban areas need to embark on a cluster of cities approach to spatial planning and infrastructure investments.

---

[161] ADB. 2019. *Strategy 2030. Operational Plan for Priority 4: Making Cities More Livable, 2019–2024.* Manila.

[162] An FUA consists of a city and its commuting zone. FUAs therefore consist of a densely inhabited city and a less densely populated commuting zone whose labor market is highly integrated with the city. See: Organization for Economic Cooperation and Development. Functional Urban Areas by Country.

At the urban level, instruments and investments need to support compact development. Resolution 335 encourages a compact urban form in the central cores of Tajikistan's largest cities, but it is unknown if it will be able to completely reverse low-density development from being the dominant spatial pattern. The price per square meter of units in high-rise buildings in central areas is significantly higher than single-story typologies in the periphery, and the limited access to long-term financing makes these units harder to afford. The development of mortgage finance at an affordable rate and the simplification of the approval regime as well as incentives for developers to engage in affordable housing will be key enablers of the transition to compact urban development.

Policy Measures: Setting the Pathway for a Livable Urban Development Model

National Level

Establishing an urbanization strategy. The NDS has identified urbanization as an instrument for regional growth. It mentions the development of a system of small towns, medium-sized cities, and large agglomerations to create spatially distributed poles of growth that broaden access to opportunities and reinforce the role of secondary urban areas. Developing a system of cities requires a national-level strategy for urbanization that will (i) integrate urbanization into the national growth agenda, linking it with economic development policies and actions as well as measures to engage the private sector in land and infrastructure, (ii) develop a national strategy and long-term spatial development program that identifies economic centers to balance access to opportunities and services, and (iii) identify the reforms required in the urban planning and management system so that the strategy cascades into operational spatial documents at the subnational level.

Supporting the development of an urban economy in real estate and tourism. Creating jobs in urban areas will enhance the country's capacity to retain and benefit from its full labor force rather than exporting it. Policy and infrastructure investments are required to support the development of key urban economy sectors such as real estate, construction, and tourism to increase their contribution to national GDP. The activity will consist of the preparation of a variety of measures for the improvement of the conditions for real estate development and to support the tourism development strategies currently being formulated with assistance from ADB.[163] These may include (i) enhancing tourism attractiveness in selected cities, through urban design measures for the improved presentation of tourism assets, as well as the identification of investments to close infrastructure gaps around the most-visited tourism assets; (ii) supporting value creation in the housing sector through reliable and updated information on supply and demand, prices, and costs; (iii) devising financing mechanisms that increase accessibility to mortgages; (iv) developing zoning regulations that clearly set the rules of the game and promote the engagement of private sector developers in an organized manner and in accordance with urban planning objectives; (v) streamlining the construction permit process based on zoning

---

[163] ADB. 2023. Tajikistan: Tourism Development Project.

regulations and systematizing the process of transfer of land use rights for additional transparency; and (vi) promoting the digitalization of the construction industry, specifically introducing urban planning tools and processes and city management dashboards.

Regional Level

Strengthening spatial planning at the regional level. The action will support regional development by identifying Tajikistan's system of cities, derived from the primary urban clusters of Dushanbe, Khujand, Bokhtar, and Kulob. To provide critical inputs in preparing downstream urban planning documents, it will come out with a regional- and/or city-level development road map that (i) defines an analytical unit of study for primary clusters of cities (for example, using the FUA concept) and other economically relevant areas and settlements types, such as along transport corridors, trade nodes, and economic zones; (ii) identifies comparative advantages and complementary economic activities in the clusters; (iii) prepares a gap analysis of the available services and social amenities in each cluster; and (iv) identifies investments that improve the connectivity between the settlements that form the clusters and hinterland agricultural districts.

Urban Level

Supporting the transition to a more livable urban development model. The implementation of Resolution 335, which requires a minimum height of five stories in new buildings, will increase the population density at the core of major urban areas. The current urban planning framework and infrastructure networks do not seem ready to enable such transformation. This will be addressed through the preparation of an action plan for compact urban development in Dushanbe that will support relevant municipal departments, the Committee on Architecture and Construction (CAC), and other stakeholders to make short-term decisions while providing input to the preparation of the next update of general plans, detailed plans, and the construction strategy. The action plans for a more livable compact spatial development may include modules to (i) adjust land-use planning with measures to minimize travel demand, promoting mixed-use development and the proximity of residential areas to productive and commercial ones; (ii) introduce zoning regulations and incentives for prioritizing urban redevelopment over greenfield projects; (iii) increase readiness to climate change through mapping of risk exposure to natural hazards and climate impacts including heat island effects and floods; (iv) improve air quality through specific action plans;[164] (v) plan and manage a system of green cover and open spaces; and (vi) develop standards for energy-efficient urban housing and other buildings.

---

[164] Clean Air Action for Bishkek, the Kyrgyz Republic and Almaty, Kazakhstan, under ADB Regional Technical Assistance 9919: Integrated and Innovative Solutions for More Livable Cities, can be used as a reference.

Investments: Demonstrating the Livable Urban Development Model

Transport and mobility

Indicative knowledge and preparatory support technical assistance:

- Travel demand forecasts at national and regional levels to inform the preparation of a sector master plan, and establish a method for periodic review and update to adjust investment programming
- Sustainable Urban Mobility Plans for Tajikistan's largest cities, Dushanbe, Khujand, Bokhtar and Kulob, at FUA scale
- Action plan for the transition of *marshrutka* operators into an integral part of the public transport system, including fare, route, and fleet integration
- E-mobility policy and corresponding regulatory framework; identification of cities to implement pilot electric vehicle infrastructure
- Public–private partnership (PPP) opportunities in the delivery of public transport and mobility projects

Indicative investments:

- Viability studies in Dushanbe and potentially other cities for mass transport systems, (e.g., bus rapid transport) including dedicated lane infrastructure and energy efficient rolling stock
- Construction of active mobility infrastructure, including streetscape design, pedestrian and bike lanes, and proximity public spaces
- Upgrade of tertiary roads and traffic management improvement, including for example the conversion of narrow two-way secondary and tertiary streets into one-way streets, and integration with intelligent street parking management systems
- Development of model park-and-ride facilities at selected city traffic gateways, as well as a regulatory mechanism for generating potential revenues for public transport and mixed-use development
- Pilot electric vehicle infrastructure in selected cities

Water supply and sanitation and solid waste management

Indicative knowledge and preparatory support technical assistance:

- Quantitative analytics and support for the development of a sector master plan
- Introduction and operationalization of the smart management system and integration of customer databases, billing, collection, accounting and reporting in SUE *Dushanbevodokanal*
- Strengthening the institutional, technical, and financial capacity and efficiency of the water supply and sanitation of SUE *Dushanbevodokanal*, including the elaboration of a sustainable business model and nonrevenue water reduction program

- PPP opportunities for the provision of municipal infrastructure and management of urban services

Indicative investments:

- Area-based investments in basic urban infrastructure and services such as water supply and sanitation, sewerage, and waste management in specific locations of the largest cities to enable compact urban development as well as around the most-visited urban tourism assets
- Rehabilitation of existing water and sewerage infrastructure, including wells, water storages, pumping stations, water metering system, and transmission pipes in Dushanbe
- Sewerage and stormwater networks in cities of flood-prone regions
- Solid waste collection points, management, and processing plants in large cities

Climate mitigation and adaptation

Indicative knowledge and preparatory support technical assistance:

- Emissions inventory
- Assessment of the applicability of nature-based solutions and sponge city approaches to address urban flooding issues and application to urban water streams
- Identification of environment improvement projects including urban forestation and ecosystem restoration
- Assessment of circular economy opportunities and road map for a built environment sector policy

Indicative investments:

- Air quality monitoring systems including hardware and data analysis methods
- Pilot sponge city approaches in selected cities and urban fringes to protect floodplains, restore wetlands, and create landscaped spaces along riverfronts and wetlands
- Pilot compact city upgrades including the preparation of recommendations and/or updated documents (codes, norms, and standards) to facilitate the transition to a greener urban planning process, such as the design and implementation of model public space network and green upgrade projects to be deployed in high-density, mixed-use areas in selected large cities

Urban tourism

Indicative knowledge and preparatory support technical assistance:

- Assessment of the potential for urban tourism and identification of priority cities using as input the market demand characterization included in the ongoing ADB Tajikistan Tourism Development Project, particularly in the historical and cultural tourism categories identified in the Tajikistan National Strategy for Tourism Development 2018
- Preparation of tourism master plans for selected cities defining historic urban landscapes, including urban infrastructure (access roads, urban services, and public space) and amenities and beautification to improve the areas to acceptable standards; adapting zoning and building codes to cultural heritage conservation; and enhancing marketing and promotion strategies

Indicative investments:

- Development of area-based beautification pilots in selected cities, including accessibility (last-mile access roads to tourism destinations and universal design); streetscapes to enhance walkability with adequate urban furniture, lighting and other amenities; improvement of tourist-related urban environmental services; and enhancement of tourism management through an urban tourism certification program, information facilities, and vocational training for small tourism businesses and service providers

Housing

Indicative knowledge and preparatory support technical assistance:

- Development of a housing sector master plan
- Assessment of incentives for private sector developers and investment funds to engage in the construction of high-rise affordable housing, identifying required regulatory framework reforms
- Assessment of incentives to home buyers, including access to the mortgage market in coordination with the banking sector

Indicative investments:

- Provision of secured loans to private sector developers to partially finance the construction and finalization of affordable, cost-efficient apartments in high-rise buildings and residential complexes that cater to low/low-middle income populations[165]

---

[165] For example, ADB's M Square Affordable Housing Project in Georgia.

Integration of digital technology

Indicative knowledge and preparatory support technical assistance:

- Preparation of a national digitalization strategy linked to urbanization
- Preparation of a Smart Dushanbe action plan and identification of pilot projects

Indicative investments:

- Pilot intelligent street parking management systems
- Pilot intelligent transport systems
- Dashboard and control center for smart city management

Skills: Developing the governance of the livable urbanization model

Strengthening the governance of functional urban areas. The shift to the scope of an FUA, the transition to market land development, and the delivery of a compact spatial pattern are likely to be a challenge for the urban planning and city management departments of municipal governments. These will also need stronger coordination between central level and city governments. The update of urban planning instruments will require an adjustment period for technical staff on, among other approaches, making evidence-based decisions integrating sector programs and introducing structured citizen participation processes and a gender perspective. The pathway to digitalization needs to be laid out for the creation of a system for storage, provision, and publication in electronic form of documents on urban planning and the construction permitting process, which requires that systems are modernized and urban planning departments equipped with data generation capacities and digital technologies.

Supporting municipal financial sustainability. This will be done through capacity development in budgeting, enhancing transparency of intergovernmental fiscal relations, and the improvement of own-source revenue and tax collection. The National Development Strategy (NDS) identified local government development as a priority thus all these issues could be included in a future reform program for local governments via a rules-based transparent transfer system to foster efficiency and prevent abrupt disruptions to the income that municipalities and subnational governments (SNGs) expect to receive.

Potential policy measures and investments proposed for the short term are summarized below (Table 26).

Table 26: Proposed Policy Measures and Indicative Investments, Short-Term Scenario (1–5 Years)

Policy Measures **Objective: Set pathway for livable urban development model.**	
National	Put in place an urbanization strategy • Integrate urbanization in national growth agenda • Develop national strategy and long-term spatial development program • Identify reforms required in urban planning and management system to cascade strategy and operations to subnational level Support the development of an urban economy in real estate and tourism • Enhance tourism attractiveness in selected cities • Support value creation in housing sector • Devise financing mechanisms to increase access to mortgage • Enhance zoning regulations • Streamline construction permit process • Promote digitalization of construction industry
Regional	Strengthen spatial planning through preparation of a regional- and/or city-level development road map • Define unit of analysis for clusters of cities • Identify comparative advantages and complementary economic activities in city clusters • Analyze gaps in available services and social amenities in each cluster • Identify investments to improve connectivity of city clusters and hinterland agricultural districts
Urban	Support transition to livable urban development through compact development action plan and demonstration model in Dushanbe • Adjust land-use planning to minimize travel demand and promote mixed-use and proximity of residential, commercial, and work spaces • Introduce zoning regulations and incentives for prioritizing urban redevelopment over greenfield projects • Increase climate readiness through risk mapping • Improve air quality through specific action plans • Plan and manage a system of green cover and open spaces • Develop standards for energy-efficient urban housing and other buildings
Technical Assistance and Indicative Investments **Objective: Demonstrate livable urban development model.**	
Transport and mobility	Knowledge and preparatory support technical assistance • Travel demand forecasts (national and regional) • Sustainable urban mobility plans, FUA scale (5 largest cities) • Action planning: Integration of *marshrutka* into public transport system • E-mobility policy and regulatory framework • PPP opportunities

continued on next page

Table 26 *continued*

Technical Assistance and Indicative Investments **Objective: Demonstrate livable urban development model.**	
	Investments • Mass transport systems viability studies (Dushanbe, possibly other cities) • Construction of active mobility infrastructure, including streetscape design, pedestrian and bike lanes, and proximity public spaces • Upgrade of tertiary roads and traffic management improvement • Model park-and-ride facilities (selected city traffic gateways) • Pilot electric vehicle infrastructure (selected cities)
Water supply and sanitation and solid waste management	Knowledge and preparatory support technical assistance • Quantitative analytics and sector master plan • Smart management system (including improving billing, collection, and improving financial systems at DVK • Institutional, technical, and financial capacity building (DVK) • PPP opportunities Investments • Construction of area-based water supply, sewerage, and waste management infrastructure (5 largest cities and most visited urban tourism assets) • Rehabilitation of existing water and sewerage infrastructure (Dushanbe) • Sewerage and stormwater networks (flood-prone cities) • Solid waste collection points and processing plants (large cities)
Climate mitigation and adaptation	Knowledge and preparatory support technical assistance • Emissions inventory • Applicability of nature-based solutions and sponge city approaches to address urban flooding issues and application to urban water streams • Identification of environment improvement projects (e.g., urban forestation and ecosystem restoration) • Circular economy opportunities and road map for a built environment sector policy Investments • Air quality monitoring systems • Pilot sponge city approaches (selected cities and urban fringes) • Pilot compact city upgrades, e. g., model public space network and green upgrade (selected large cities)
Housing	Knowledge and preparatory support technical assistance • Housing sector master plan • Incentives to support high-rise affordable housing • Incentives to support access to mortgage market Investments • Secured loans for partial financing of affordable, cost-efficient apartments in high-rise buildings

continued on next page

Table 26 continued

Technical Assistance and Indicative Investments Objective: Demonstrate livable urban development model.	
Integration of Digital Technology in Urban Management	Knowledge and preparatory support technical assistance • Preparation of national digitalization strategy linked to urbanization • Smart Dushanbe action planning (including identification of pilot projects) Investments • Pilot intelligent street parking management systems • Pilot intelligent transport systems • Dashboard and control center for smart city management

DVK = *Dushanbevodokanal* State Unitary Enterprise, FUA = functional urban area, PPP = public–private partnership.

Source: Authors.

5.2 Medium Term

In the medium-term scenario (5–10 years), Tajikistan rolls out the system of cities that enables the transition to a land-linked economy. There is an increased attention to resilience, environmental protection, digitalization, and the introduction of circular economy approaches. This builds upon the policy foundation and the demonstration projects that were the focus of short-term actions, which are expected to have created consensus and momentum on urbanization as a driver of the growth agenda.

Regional development requires consistent policy and investment actions. Enabling the clusters of cities and settlements to follow a more balanced territorial development will require political support for the implementation of the regional plans, continued strengthening of the local government, and development of regional infrastructure linking the FUAs of Dushanbe, Khujand, Bokhtar, and Kulob and other areas identified in the regional plans with their hinterlands. The improvement of the road and rail transport connectivity between the clusters and economic activity nodes such as industrial and mining areas, border trade, and economic zones will enable the rural population and those living in smaller cities to access services, welfare, and employment opportunities. This will, in turn, allow the capture of the demographic window of opportunity with alternatives to both temporary and permanent migration.

Policies: Expanding the livable urban model to a system of cities

Regional Level

Developing spatial plans and subsector master plans for clusters of cities. Capitalizing on strengthened spatial planning at the regional level, this action will consist of preparing (i) spatial plans for the clusters that have been identified; (ii) subsector master plans for transport corridors (roads, railways, and air) to improve the connectivity between settlements within the clusters, and between clusters and neighboring countries, locating land and facilities for economic activity; (iii) investment programs for priority transport corridors and their associated infrastructure; and (iv) investment programs for logistics and trade centers and border terminals throughout the country.[166]

Urban Level

Preparing general plans for functional urban areas. This action consists of technical and capacity support for relevant municipal departments and the CAC to prepare general plans and detailed plans where necessary, for prioritized FUAs. The preparation will build on the experience gained in the action plan for the livable and compact development of Dushanbe, expected to have introduced an updated approach to urban planning that is multidimensional, realistic, clear-cut, and conscious of the need to deliver at pace. The general plans will apply approaches and tools such as integrated land use and transport planning, zoning regulations, vulnerability mapping, and other inputs that need to come together in a binding plan. It will also systematize and scale up demonstration projects proven successful, including nature-based solutions, sponge city approaches, area-based urban beautification projects, smart city applications for parking and traffic management, and other short-term pilots. The action will support inclusive and participatory planning techniques to activate the dialogue between stakeholders, relevant authorities, and design institutes in charge of plan preparation. The public consultation process is expected to give special attention to historic area conservation and the adaptive reuse of historic buildings, the preservation of green natural areas, and the design of public space.

Investments: Developing cluster of cities

Transport

Indicative knowledge and preparatory support technical assistance:

- Development and implementation of transport subsector master plan
- Preparation of transport connectivity plans at a cluster level

Indicative investments:

- Road corridors at a cluster scale
- Logistics facilities in borders and across regions
- Intermodal public transport stations of cluster scale with park-and-ride facilities and associated social infrastructure facilities and commercial real estate development
- electric vehicle infrastructure in pilot clusters and key corridors

---

[166] For more details, see ADB. 2021. *Tajikistan Transport Sector Assessment*. Manila.

Water supply and sanitation and solid waste management

Indicative knowledge and preparatory support technical assistance:

- Development and implementation of subsector master plan
- Scaled up introduction and operationalization of the smart management system and integration of customer databases, billing, collection, accounting, and reporting for selected municipal water supply and wastewater companies
- Strengthening the institutional, technical, and financial capacity of selected water supply and sanitation municipal companies, including sustainable business model and nonrevenue water reduction program
- Identification of PPP opportunities for the provision of municipal infrastructure and management of urban services

Indicative investments:

- City-cluster-scale investments in water supply and sanitation, sewerage, and waste management infrastructure and services in specific locations to enable compact urban development as well as around the most-visited urban tourism assets
- Rehabilitation of existing water and sewerage infrastructure, including wells, water storages, pumping stations, water metering system, and transmission pipes
- Expanded sewerage and stormwater networks in cities in flood-prone regions
- Solid waste collection processing plants and landfills in selected city clusters

Housing

Indicative investments:

- Area-based model regeneration projects in prioritized FUAs, delivering compact, affordable, low-carbon, climate-resilient, and livable eco-districts, engaging private sector investment

Integration of digital technology

Indicative investments:

- Rollout of intelligent street parking management systems in prioritized FUAs
- Rollout of intelligent transport systems
- Dashboards for city management
- Digitalization of parcel-based spatial land information
- Digitalization of the construction permits process

Resilience, climate change, and circular economy

Indicative knowledge and preparatory support technical assistance:

- Data analytics in urban and building design and operation stages to understand the impact of the introduction of circular economy parameters
- Support to the implementation of the construction industry strategy including the update of codes and the introduction of incentive packages for using recycled or locally sourced construction materials
- Identification of incentives for the reuse of land and rehabilitation of abandoned or contaminated brownfields, as well as to reduce the need for carbon-intensive mobility
- Change management and behavior shift toward the circular economy
- Embedding nature-based solutions and biodiversity (green master plans, green action plans) for protection of green spaces and ecosystems, improving flood management, and reducing urban heat islands

Potential policy measures and investments recommended for the medium term are summarized below (Table 27).

Table 27: Proposed Policy Measures and Indicative Investments, Medium-Term Scenario (5–10 Years)

Policy Measures	
Objective: Expand livable urban model to a system of cities.	
Regional Level	Develop spatial plans and subsector master plans for clusters of cities • Spatial plans for identified clusters • Subsector master plans for transport corridors (roads, railways, and air) • Investment programs for priority transport corridors • Investment programs for logistics and trade centers and border terminals throughout Tajikistan
Urban	Prepare general plans for functional urban areas. • Apply approaches and tools proven effective in first 5 years (e.g., integrated land use and transport planning, zoning regulations, vulnerability mapping) • Systematize and scale up demonstration projects proven successful (e.g., nature-based solutions, sponge city approaches, area-based urban beautification projects, smart city applications in parking and traffic management) • Support inclusive and participatory planning techniques (e.g., public consultations on historic area conservation, adaptive reuse of historic buildings, preservation of green natural areas, and design of public space)
Technical Assistance and Indicative Investments	
Objective: Develop cluster of cities.	
Transport and mobility	Knowledge and preparatory support technical assistance • Transport subsector master plan • Transport connectivity plans at cluster level • Spatial plans for identified clusters

continued on next page

Table 27 continued

	Technical Assistance and Indicative Investments Objective: Develop cluster of cities.
	Investments • Road corridors (cluster scale) • Logistics facilities (borders and regions) • Intermodal public transport stations with park-and-ride facilities (cluster scale) • Electric vehicle infrastructure (pilot clusters and key corridors)
Water supply and sanitation and solid waste management	Indicative knowledge and preparatory support technical assistance • Water supply and sanitation subsector master plan • Scaled up smart management system • Institutional, technical, and financial capacity (selected water supply and sanitation municipal companies) • PPP opportunities (municipal infrastructure and services) Investments • Water supply and sanitation, sewerage, and waste management infrastructure and services in specific locations (cluster city scale) • Rehabilitation of existing water and sewerage infrastructure • Expanded sewerage and stormwater networks (flood-prone cities) • Solid waste collection processing plants and landfills (selected city clusters)
Housing	Investments • Area-based model regeneration projects in prioritized FUAs
Integration of digital technology in urban management	Investments • Rollout of intelligent street parking management systems in prioritized FUAs • Rollout of intelligent transport systems • Dashboards for city management • Digitalization of parcel-based spatial land information • Digitalization of the construction permits process
Resilience, climate change, and circular economy	Indicative knowledge and preparatory support technical assistance • Data analytics in urban and building design and operation • Implementation of the construction industry strategy including the update of codes and the introduction of incentive packages for use of recycled or locally sourced construction materials • Incentives for reuse of land, rehabilitation of abandoned or contaminated brownfields, and reduced carbon-intensive mobility • Change management and behavior shift toward circular economy • Nature-based solutions, protection of green spaces and ecosystems, improved flood management, and urban heat island reduction measures

FUA = functional urban area, PPP = public–private partnership.
Source: Authors.

5.3 Long Term

In the long-term scenario (10–20 years), Tajikistan is recognized for consistent and sustained application of a livable urban development model that has elevated the quality of development across leading and lagging regions. The model has contributed to capturing the demographic dividend, generating employment and welfare, thus making migration a less attractive alternative.

Dushanbe is known for its livable, green, and resilient characteristics. This will have been enabled by an effective planning and governance framework and by the universal coverage and efficiency of its basic services. The city is an important node of regional stature in a network that connects with other capitals and major cities in Central Asia. Successful pilot applications in compact urban development, mobility, and smart city arrangements, among others, have been scaled up and streamlined into policy, public investment, and business practices. Housing options are accessible for all income levels in compact urban centers across Tajikistan, which attract economic, social, and cultural activities. Sprawl is marginal. Domestic and international private sector investment in land, property, and infrastructure are largely contributing to the success of the model.

Prospects for regional economic integration between Tajikistan and its neighbors in CAREC are flourishing. The improved national and regional connectivity has enabled a functional system of cities and contributed to addressing regional constraints. Secondary cities and their hinterlands are grouped in competitive clusters, making them better placed to drive economic and social returns. Human development and inequality indicators have improved on the back of a diversified and connected economy. Tourism, logistics, and other activities are on a pathway to maturity. Local governance has reached international standards in terms of budgeting and urban planning and management. The value of environmental and cultural heritage assets is widely recognized, and preservation, restoration, and adaptive reuse are mainstream practices. The circular economy model is the norm, and cities and industries meet their needs with renewable resources.

Policies: Expanding the livable urban model to the built environment sector

Embedding circular economy principles in the built environment supply chain. Urbanization in Tajikistan can spearhead a trajectory toward circularity because urban policy and infrastructure are key levers in the shift away from a linear pattern. Urbanization can be expected to increase the demand for raw materials, but an updated Construction Code can incentivize the circular use of materials for construction and manufacturing. The application of the code can also lead to a reduction in energy usage in buildings. The new generation of general plans can apply circularity to the use of land, water, and energy, guiding development toward the reuse and redevelopment of land in brownfield sites and thus supporting a compact spatial pattern that reduces mobility demands. Land and water management combined can result in the collection, storage, and reuse of rainwater, increasing resilience to climate change-induced hazards.

Investments: Achieving Livability Standards in All Regions

Transport

Indicative investments:

- Rail subsector reform and infrastructure investment program in main and spur lines, multimodal terminals, including options for infrastructure ownership and railway operations
- Network of national and local roads connecting remote and mountainous areas
- Restructuring air transport and the network of domestic airports, introducing regular domestic flights to routes other than Dushanbe–Khujand
- Expansion and further modernization of the network of logistic centers

Water supply and sanitation and solid waste management

Indicative knowledge and preparatory support technical assistance:

- Institutional, technical, and financial strengthening of other municipal and community communal service companies

Indicative investments:

- Expand service coverage to towns and settlements

Land development and housing

- Preserve land for agriculture and retain agricultural area throughout
- Regenerate urban centers that attract economic, social, and cultural activities

Circular economy

- Transition of agro-industrial clusters and enterprises in garment and footwear production in Tajikistan to circular economy approaches
- Implementation of zero waste programs[167]

Potential policy measures and investments proposed for the long term are outlined in Table 28.

---

[167] According to Zero Waste International Alliance, zero waste is "the conservation of all resources by means of responsible production, consumption, reuse, and recovery of products, packaging, and materials without burning and with no discharges to land, water, or air that threaten the environment or human health."

Table 28: Proposed Policy Measures and Indicative Investments, Long-Term Scenario (10–20 Years)

Policy Measures
Objective: Expand livable urban model to the built environment sector.
Embed circular economy principles in built environment supply chain • Incentivize circular use of materials for construction and manufacturing • Reuse and redevelop land in brownfield sites • Enhance land and water management to increase resilience to climate change-induced hazards.

Technical Assistance and Indicative Investments	
Objective: Achieve livability standards in all regions.	
Transport and mobility	Investments • Rail subsector reform and infrastructure investment program • Network of national and local roads connecting remote and mountainous areas • Restructuring of air transport and strengthening of network of domestic airports • Expansion and further modernization of the network of logistic centers
Water supply and sanitation and solid waste management	Indicative knowledge and preparatory support technical assistance • Institutional, technical, and financial strengthening of other municipal and community communal service companies Investments • Expand service coverage to towns and settlements
Land Development and Housing	Investments • Preserve land for agriculture and retain a similar percentage • Regenerate urban centers that attract economic, social, and cultural activities.
Circular economy	• Transition of agro-industrial clusters and enterprises in garment and footwear production in Tajikistan to circular economy approaches • Implementation of zero waste programs

Source: Authors.

5.4 Applicability and Relevance of Innovative Solutions

Mortgages and access to finance. The mortgage rate in Tajikistan is the highest, not only in Central Asia, but in all post-Soviet countries—in the national currency it is 22%–26%.[168] Banks that offer mortgages have almost similar conditions, such as 30% down payment with a tenure of up to 10 years. Limited assistance from the state in subsidizing concessional mortgages could improve this issue. Alternatively, international financial institutions (IFIs) including ADB, could provide concessional loans to local commercial banks for further on-lending to mortgage housing at lower and/or affordable rates.

---

[168] In the Russian Federation, it is 8%–10%; in Kazakhstan, 13%; and in Uzbekistan and the Kyrgyz Republic, 15%–20%.

Partnerships with the private sector and foundations to leverage resources and attract private sector financing. The Law of the Republic of Tajikistan "On Public–Private Partnership" was adopted on 28 December 2012. The law specifies two types of projects that can be implemented under PPP: (i) infrastructure projects, including design, construction, development, and use of a new infrastructure facility or reconstruction, modernization, extension, and operation of any existing infrastructure facility; and (ii) social services project, design, development, and operation of any structure operating under the jurisdiction of the state partner before the start of the project that directly or indirectly provides social services to the population for not less than 3 years (domestic, psychological, medical, educational, and other services).

Current and potential PPP initiatives include:

- The toll road between Dushanbe and Chanak on the border with Uzbekistan has been in operation since 2010. Tolling is currently managed by the company Innovative Road Solution LTD.
- In April 2021, the Municipality of Dushanbe invited legal and individual entities, both domestic and foreign, to participate in the construction of the new Dushanbe Zoo under a PPP arrangement. However, this was postponed due to the COVID-19 pandemic.
- Other potential PPP projects with developers include the construction of public amenities in exchange for land use rights or buildability bonuses. Under this scheme, for example, a developer will get the right to build a whole residential block with schools, kindergarten, primary health care facilities, public spaces, etc., while they could sell the residences and shops, but transfer public amenities to the municipality at no charge.
- Low tariffs in services such as wastewater treatment, water supply, public transport, and hospitals has so far hindered the interest of the private sector to engage in partnerships.

Experience with on-lending mechanisms. Municipal communal service companies in water and wastewater, solid waste management, public transport, and other areas have borrowed directly from IFIs under sovereign guarantee and project support agreements with the municipality.[169] Sometimes, the the Ministry of Finance (MOF) borrows from the IFI and on-lends to these companies at a very small fee or no fee.

Potential for fund flow arrangements through alternative sub-sovereign mechanisms, such as private or public financial institutions and/or intermediaries not particularly requiring sovereign guarantees and other state obligations, will enable private companies to attract both domestic and international investments using PPP arrangements; however, the tariff policy needs to be adjusted to market requirements and/or subsidized by the municipality to meet cost recovery.

---

[169] State or municipal company borrows from investor and MOF provides sovereign guarantee to pay back to investor the loan and interest in case of company's default. Project support agreement is an agreement with the municipality, where the municipality ensures that services provided by the company are paid within their jurisdiction.

Appendixes

Appendix 1: Main Legal Documents on Public Finance Management

- "On Public Finances of the Republic of Tajikistan" (2011 with amendments in 2013, 2016, and 2018)
- "On State and State Guaranteed Borrowing and Debt" (2021)
- "On Internal Audit of the Public Sector" (2010 with amendments in 2016 and 2020)
- "On Financial Management and Internal Financial Control in the Public Sector" (2010)
- "On Accounting and Financial Reporting" (2011)
- "On the Chamber of Accounts of the Republic of Tajikistan" (2011)
- "On the National Bank of Tajikistan" (1996 with changes in 2007)
- "On Banking Activities" (2009)
- "On the State Financial Control in the Republic of Tajikistan" (2002 with changes in 2007)
- "On Investments" (2007)
- "On State Registration of Legal Entities and Individual Entrepreneurs" (2009)
- "On Licensing of Separate Types of Activities" (as amended in 2006)
- The Tax Code (2022)
- Customs Code (2004)
- Law on the State Budget for 2013 (2012)
- The Law on the State Budget for 2014 (2013)
- The Law on the State Budget for 2015 (2014)
- The Law on the State Budget for 2016 (2015)
- The Law on the State Budget for 2017 (2016)
- The Law on the State Budget for 2018 (2017)
- The Law on the State Budget for 2019 (2018)
- The Law on the State Budget for 2020 (2019)
- The Law on the State Budget for 2021 (2020)

- "On Public Procurement of Goods, Works and Services", 24 February 2006, No. 184, (as amended by the Act of 16 April 2012, No. 815)
- Guidelines for Public Procurement Procedures. Approved by Order of the Ministry of Economic Development and Trade of the Republic of Tajikistan on January 17, registered with the Ministry of Justice of the Republic of Tajikistan on February 11, 2008, No. 357
- Decree of the Government dated 1 July 2007 No. 319 "On the establishment of a Qualification Commission in defining and award status of 'qualified procuring entity' "
- Decree of the Government No. 500 dated October 2, 2010, "On approval of the Rules for opening of bid proposal for procurement of goods, works and services in state investment projects in the Republic of Tajikistan"

Appendix 2: Select Urban Projects and Urban-Related Activities of International Financial Institutions

World Bank

Year	Project ID	Project Name	Status
2022	P177563	Additional Financing to Power Utility Financial Recovery Project	Active
2022	P175356	Tajikistan Strengthening Water and Irrigation Management Project	Active
2022	P177325	Tajikistan Water Supply and Sanitation Investment Project	Active
2022	P177779	Tajikistan Preparedness and Resilience to Disasters Project	Active
2021	P177780	Additional Financing and Restructuring of the Tajikistan COVID-19 Project	Active
2021	P175952	Strengthening Resilience of the Agriculture Sector Project	Active
2021	P173977	Modernizing the National Statistical System in Tajikistan	Active
2021	P171892	Tax Reform Operation	Active
2021	P175456	Additional Financing to Rural Electrification Project	Active
2021	P175168	Additional Financing for the Tajikistan Emergency COVID-19 Project	Active
2021	P176216	Additional Financing for the Tajikistan Emergency COVID-19 Project	Active
2020	P172924	Additional Financing for Public Finance Management Modernization Project 2	Active
2020	P169168	Early Childhood Development to Build Tajikistan's Human Capital Project	Active
2020	P173765	Tajikistan Emergency COVID-19 Project	Active
2020	P168211	Tajikistan Power Utility Financial Recovery	Active
2019	P171248	Support for Preparation of the Rural Electrification, Sebzor Hydro Power Plant, and Khorog-Qozideh Power Transmission Line Projects	Active
2019	P170132	Rural Electrification Project	Active
2019	P168326	Rural Economy Development Project	Active
2019	P163734	Dushanbe Water Supply and Wastewater Project	Active
2019	P162637	Rural Water Supply and Sanitation Project	Active
2018	P165831	Social Safety Net Strengthening Project	Active
2017	P158499	Agriculture Commercialization Project—Additional Financing	Active
2017	P158298	Strengthening Critical Infrastructure against Natural Hazards	Active
2016	P154561	Real Estate Registration Project	Closed
2015	P153709	Environmental Land Management and Rural Livelihoods—Additional Financing	Closed
2015	P154729	Tajikistan Second Dushanbe Water Supply Project— Additional Financing	Active
2015	P150381	Public Finance Management Modernization Project 2	Active
2015	P133449	Communal Services Development Fund	Closed
2014	P126997	Tajikistan: Extractive Industries Transparency Initiative Implementation	Closed
2014	P132652	Tajikistan Agriculture Commercialization Project	Closed
2013	P147860	Improving Social Accountability in the Water Sector	Closed
2013	P126130	Tajikistan Health Services Improvement Project	Active

continued on next page

Appendix 2 *continued*

Year	Project ID	Project Name	Status
2013	P122694	Environmental Land Management and Rural Livelihoods Project	Closed
2013	P133191	Tajikistan—Public Procurement Capacity Building	Closed
2012	P126042	Tajikistan PDPG6	Closed
2012	P127807	Tax Administration	Closed
2012	P130091	Private Sector Competitiveness	Closed
2012	P127130	Additional Financing Municipal Infrastructure	Closed
2012	P129313	Additional Financing Land Registration & Cadastre System for Sustainable Agriculture Project	Closed
2012	P122141	Additional Financing Energy Loss Reduction	Closed
2012	P130702	Tajikistan Public Sector Accounting Reform Project	Closed
2011	P118196	Second Dushanbe Water Supply Project	Closed
2011	P120445	Tajikistan's Fifth Programmatic Development Policy Grant	Closed
2011	P123704	Tajikistan Government-Implemented Grant for Targeting and Payment of Social Assistance	Closed
2010	P121811	Community & Basic Health Project Additional Financing—2	Closed
2010	P119690	Public Employment For Sustainable Agriculture And Water Management Project	Closed
2010	P117692	PDPG 4	Closed
2010	P118430	Additional Financing—Ferghana Valley Water Resources Management Project	Closed
2010	P120834	Energy Emergency—Additional Financing	Closed
2010	P115343	Fast Track Initiative Catalytic Fund Grant—3	Closed
2009	P099840	Public Financial Management Modernization	Closed
2009	P115801	Community and Basic Health Project—Additional Financing	Closed
2009	P106963	PDPG 3	Closed
2008	P112136	Community & Basic Health Additional Financing	Closed
2008	P110555	Energy Emergency Project	Closed
2007	P104006	Tajikistan Youth Social and Economic Opportunity Grant	Closed
2007	P096930	PDPG 2	Closed
2006	P101592	Additional Financing for the Dushanbe Water Supply Project	Closed
2006	P074889	PDPG	Closed
2006	P096861	Public Sector Reform Technical Assistance	Closed
2006	P098410	Strengthening the National Statistical System	Closed
2006	P079027	Municipal Infrastructure Development Project	Closed
2005	P084035	Ferghana Valley Water Resources Management Project	Closed
2005	P089244	Energy Loss Reduction Project	Closed
2005	P089566	Land Registration & Cadastre System for Sustainable Agriculture Project	Closed
2002	P057883	Dushanbe Water Supply Project	Closed
Pipeline	P177475	Learning Environment—Foundation of Quality Education	Pipeline

continued on next page

Appendix 2 *continued*

Year	Project ID	Project Name	Status
Pipeline	P176602	Sugd Private Solar Power Project	Pipeline
Pipeline	P171382	Tajikistan Digital Foundations Project	Pipeline
Pipeline	P177930	Resilient and Sustainable Tajikistan Development Policy Operations	Pipeline
Pipeline	P178878	Tajikistan Social Protection Systems Modernization and Emergency Response Project	Pipeline
Pipeline	P178261	Sugd Private Solar Guarantee	Pipeline
Pipeline	P177722	Tajikistan Financial and Private Sector Development Project	Pipeline
Pipeline	P178831	Millati Solim: Tajikistan Healthy Nation Project	Pipeline
Pipeline	P179630	Dushanbe Sustainable Urban Development Project	Pipeline
Pipeline	P178355	Additional Financing—Tajikistan Socio-Economic Resilience Strengthening Project	Pipeline
Pipeline	P178819	Technical Assistance for Financing Framework for Rogun Hydropower Project	Pipeline

COVID-19 = coronavirus disease, ID = identification number, PDPG = Programmatic Development Policy Grant.
Source: Authors, based on World Bank documents and databases.

European Bank for Reconstruction and Development

Year	Project ID	Project Name	Status
2021	52789	GrCF2 W2—Dushanbe E-Mobility	Disbursing
2021	52574	Fayzobod Water and Wastewater Project	Signed
2020	51667	Dushanbe Energy Loss Reduction Project	Disbursing
2020	49375	GrCF2 W2—Dushanbe District Heating Project	Disbursing
2020	51666	Tajikistan Energy Efficiency Framework	Approved
2019	51436	Kulob Water and Wastewater Project	Disbursing
2019	49930	Khatlon Energy Loss Reduction Project	Disbursing
2017	49083	Khatlon Public Transport	Disbursing
2016	46795	Yavan Solid Waste Sub-project	Repaying
2016	46794	Kulob Solid Waste Sub-project	Repaying
2016	47253	Qairokkum Hydro Power Plant Climate Resilience Upgrade	Repaying
2015	47477	Khujand Solid Waste Sub-project	Repaying
2015	47398	Nurek Water and Wastewater Project	Repaying
2015	47221	Cross Regional Power Trade	Repaying
2015	46288	Khujand Public Transport Project	Repaying
2015	47057	Tajik Water II—Central Water Rehabilitation	Cancelled
2014	46197	Tajikistan Solid Waste Framework	Approved
2014	47040	Tajik Water II—North Water Rehabilitation	Cancelled
2014	46409	Nurek Solid Waste Sub-project	Repaying
2014	46935	Tajik Water II—Khorog GBAO Water Rehabilitation	Repaying

continued on next page

Appendix 2 continued

Year	Project ID	Project Name	Status
2014	46147	Khorog Solid Waste Sub-Project	Repaying
2014	44753	Khujand Wastewater Project	Repaying
2013	43755	Tursun-Zade Solid Waste	Repaying
2013	43754	Kurgan-Tyube Solid Waste	Repaying
2012	43257	Khatlon Water Rehabilitation	Repaying
2012	43255	North Tajik Water Rehabilitation II	Repaying
2012	42232	Dushanbe-Uzbekistan Border Road Improvement Project	Repaying
2011	41769	Khujand Solid Waste Management Project	Repaying
2011	41642	Central Tajik Water Rehabilitation Project	Repaying
2011	41538	Sugd Energy Loss Reduction project	Repaying
2009	39989	Dushanbe Public Transport	Repaying
2008	38901	Dushanbe Solid Waste Management Project	Repaying
2007	36826	Road Maintenance Development Project	Repaying
2004	34583	Khujand Water Supply Improvement Project	Completed

ID = identification number, GBAO = Gorno-Badakhshan Autonomous *Oblast* (Mountainous Badakhshan Autonomous Region), GrCF2 W2 = Green Cities Framework 2 Window II.

Source: Authors, based on European Bank for Reconstruction and Development documents.

www.ingramcontent.com/pod-product-compliance
Lightning Source LLC
Chambersburg PA
CBHW040930240426
43667CB00027B/3000